The Poetry Review

The Poetry Society, 22 Betterton Street, London WC2H 9BX

The Poetry Review

The Poetry Society, 22 Betterton Street, London WC2H 9BX
Tel: +44 (0)20 7420 9880 • Fax: +44 (0)20 7240 4818
Email: poetryreview@poetrysociety.org.uk
poetrysociety.org.uk/thepoetryreview

Editor: Emily Berry
Production: Michael Sims

ISBN: 978-1-911046-07-3 ISSN: 0032 2156
Cover artwork: Manshen Lo, manshenlo.com

. . .

SUBMISSIONS
For details of our submission guidelines,
please visit poetrysociety.org.uk/thepoetryreview

ADVERTISING
To place advertisements, visit
poetrysociety.org.uk/thepoetryreview or
contact Oliver Fox on +44 (0)20 7420 9886,
email: marketing@poetrysociety.org.uk

BOOKSHOP DISTRIBUTION
Central Books, 50 Freshwater Road, London
RM8 1RX, UK. Tel: +44 (0)20 8525 8800
or visit centralbooks.com

PBS OFFER TO POETRY SOCIETY MEMBERS
The Poetry Book Society offers Poetry Society
Members a special 10% discount (plus postage)
on books bought from poetrybooks.co.uk.
For details and to obtain the discount code,
please contact Paul McGrane on
+44 (0)20 7420 9881.

SUBSCRIPTIONS & SALES
UK individuals: £35 / Europe: £45
Rest of the World: £50 (overseas delivery by airmail)
Single issue: £8.95 plus postage. Order from
poetrysociety.org.uk/shop or contact Paul McGrane
on +44 (0)20 7420 9881. Pay by cheque
(sterling and US dollar cheques only),
credit card or Direct Debit.

The Poetry Review is also available on audio CD.

The Poetry Review is the magazine of
The Poetry Society and was first published in 1912.
A subscription to *The Poetry Review* is included as
part of membership of The Poetry Society. It is also
on sale in leading bookshops. A digital version of
the magazine is also available. Views expressed in
The Poetry Review are not necessarily those of The
Poetry Society; those of individual contributors
are not necessarily those of the Editor.

Charity Commission No. 303334.

Cover quote by W.S. Graham, see p. 7

THEPOETRYSOCIETY

ARTS COUNCIL
ENGLAND

Supported using public funding by

CONTENTS

Gallery

W.S. Graham at 100   7

Poems

Fran Lock   *from* cordelia at the home for the incurables   13
Kim Hyesoon /   A Face   17
  Don Mee Choi   A Doll
                             Underworld
                             Asphyxiation
                             Don't
Jack Nicholls   Auld Lang Syne   23
Fiona Benson   Fly   25
                             Village
                             Hide and Seek
                             [Zeus] Anatomical Dolls
                             Haruspex
Hannah Lowe   Milked   31
                             Cold Stone
Doireann Ní Ghríofa   Craquelure   33
Kathryn Maris   The death of empiricism   34
                             from The House of Atreus

Manifestos

Harmony Holiday, Wendy Cope and Choman Hardi   37

Prose *from* Poetry

from 'Microliths': Paul Celan translated by Pierre Joris   45

Poems

Carolyn Jess-Cooke   We Have to Leave the Earth Because   51
                               We Know So Much
Mona Arshi   Like the first morning   52
                             Ghazal: Darkness

Jack Underwood	There Is A Supermassive Black Hole...	54
	A girl or woman in relation to either or both of her parents	
Ruth McIlroy	Change of Shift at the University Swimming Pool	56
	For example I was in the sea at 4 a.m. today	
Philip Gross	Himself	57
	The Age of Electricity	
Rebecca Goss	Reverse Charge Call	60
Alison Brackenbury	Wednesday on the 97	61
	Sheela na gig, St Michael's, Oxford	
	Directions	
Lawrence Sail	Birdcall	64
Igor Klikovac / John McAuliffe	Jovo	65
Ruth Padel	Clast	66
Anthony Anaxagorou	After the Formalities	69

Essay

I know that men can mistake: Andrew McMillan on Tom Paulin   74

Prose from Poetry

Willing to be reckless: Ange Mlinko on Marianne Moore   82

Reviews

Kayo Chingonyi on Douglas Dunn and Penelope Shuttle	96
Karen McCarthy Woolf reviews Danez Smith, Cal Freeman and Ishion Hutchinson	100
Carol Rumens on Jackie Kay, Miles Burrows and Leontia Flynn	105
So Mayer reviews the feminine poetics of Irene Solà, Shivanee Ramlochan and Khairani Barokka	110
Vidyan Ravinthiran on Stephanie Burt and Ahren Warner	115
Rory Waterman reviews Jacqueline Saphra and Roddy Lumsden	120
Claire Crowther on Sasha Dugdale and Sina Queyras	125
Jane Yeh reviews first collections by Hera Lindsay Bird, Jenna Clake and Kaveh Akbar	130
Nahrain Al-Mousawi on an anthology of new Palestinian poetry	135
The National Poetry Competition 2017 winners	140

EDITORIAL

The theme of this missive is "where are the songs of spring?" in the midst of a blizzard. On my unseasonal balcony the daffodils I bought two weeks ago are now on their knees, burying their heads in the snow. Imagine me gazing out from the highest window of a tall house over the fields to watch the bad weather rolling in, and then trying to look *beyond* that, to see if there might be any good weather on the horizon (not that I live in a tall house, nor can see any fields from my windows). "One must have a mind of winter" to do this, as our old friend Wallace Stevens advised us, and one must have a mind of winter to write from a place like that, I think, to hold the gaze of what is cold and bleak. Many of the songs in this spring issue seem to have sprung from such a place, the place where something bright yellow (the most hopeful colour there is) is submerged beneath something merciless. And this isn't T.S. Eliot's "forgetful snow", it's much more exacting. It remembers everything.

Today the sky is an impenetrable, uniform off-white, like the blank page of a Word document I've been staring into too long. The "nothing that is not there, and the nothing that is". No way in. "The hard world can be seen but not entered," writes Kim Hyesoon in Don Mee Choi's translation, "the world is white like a movie screen but with clenched fists" ('A Face'). "Is what we call the world / Punishing you more / Than me?" asks W.S. Graham in a draft poem unearthed from the archives by the editors of *The Caught Habits of Language*, an anthology celebrating this, his centenary year. How indeed do we know how one person's pain compares to another's, how differently, or samely, we experience the world? Does writing about the bad times – internal or external (even supposing the two can be distinguished) – help us get out from under them? Do we, in fact, have a duty to write about them, as Carolyn Jess-Cooke suggests in her poem 'We Have to Leave the Earth Because We Know So Much': "we have to write these things / we have to tell them to the forest / and the watchful snows." When poets write about the hard world, which they do most of the time, about illness, grief, death, injustice, about individual and collective suffering, then they do find a way into it, they chisel away some of the ice for the rest of us.

The act of writing is, I believe, a hopeful one, whatever its content: it's a message to the future where it will eventually become a message from the past. It's an acknowledgement of "the change that is bound to come" (Fran Lock), that's maybe just beyond the horizon. It's like ringing a little bell in the belief that somewhere, sometime, another bell will ring in answer. As Choman Hardi urges us in her manifesto, which celebrates the power of bearing witness, "we need to be willing to suffer, to share pain, to feel strongly." Meanwhile Jack Underwood writes reassuringly, "The story of difficulty goes that it / was experienced, then spread across / the land like a more efficient language [...] / It's natural to be overwhelmed."

Emily Berry

This issue features our annual transatlantic exchange with US magazine Poetry, *edited by Don Share. This year rather than exchanging poems we have exchanged essays (essays from* The Poetry Review *will appear in* Poetry *later this year).*

GALLERY: W.S. GRAHAM AT 100

A selection of Graham's drafts and sketches published in celebration of his centenary year

[What We Call the World]

Is what we call the world
Punishing you more
Than me? I mean is your
Threshold higher and if
So how do you know? I knew
A man who wept at blue.

A man who wept at green.
I cannot bear to be tortured.
I mean I cannot bear
To change my torture. Age
Is easing me away.
It is as though the sea

I had a relationship with
And employed so casually
Is rushing in with new
Prongs and cruel capsizes
To seek my tender places.

Typescript draft, dated 1972. Robin Skelton Special Collection, University of Victoria, British Columbia, Canada.

+ · 14 11 75

Untidy Dreadful Table

Lying with no love on the paper
Between the typing hammers I spied
Myself with looking eyes looking
Down to cover me with words.

I wont have it. I know the night
Is late here sitting at my table
But I am not a boy running
The hide and seeking streets.

I am getting on. My table now
Shuffles its papers out of reach
With last year's letters going yellow
From looking out of the window.

I sit here late and I hammer myself
On to the other side of the paper.
There I jump through all surprises ·
~~While the reader is making faces.~~

The reader and I are making faces.

I am not complaining. Some of the·faces
I see are interesting indeed.
Take your own, for example, a fine
Grimace of vessels over the bone.

~~Of course~~ I see you backwards, ~~covered~~
With ~~backward words on the other side.~~
I must tackle my dreadful table
And ~~go on the hide and seeking hill.~~

FINAL

WSG

Of course I see you backwards, covered
With words backwards from the other side.
I must tackle my dreadful table ⟵
And go on the hide and seeking hill.

WSG
14 11 75

LOCH THOM

1

Just for the sake of recovering
I walked backward from fifty-six
And managed to not trip or stumble
To find Loch Thom and turned round
To see the stretch of my childhood
Before me. Here is the loch. The same
Long-beaked cries curl across
The heather-edges of the water held
Between the hills a boyhood's walk
Up from Greenock. It is the morning.

And I am here with my mother's *mammy's*
Bramble jam scones in my pocket.
I have come some distance from the sea
Backwards to find Loch Thom maybe
In this light does not recognise me.

This is a lonely freshwater loch.
No farms on the edge. Only
Heather grouse-moor stretching
Down to Greenock and One Hope
Street or stretching away across
Into the blue moors of Ayrshire.

2

And almost I am back again
Wading the heather down to the edge
To sit. The minnows go by in shoals
Like iron-filings in the shallows.

My mother is dead. My father is dead
And all the trout I used to know
Leaping from their sad rings are dead.

3

age

I drop my crumbs into the shallow
Weed for the minnows and pinheads.
You see that I will have to rise
And turn round and get back where
My running home will slow for a moment
To let me on. It is a colder
Stretch of water than I remember.

The curlew's cry travelling still
Kills me fairly and the weeping
Crested lapwing will see me away.
Still unshot by human hand
The grouse flurry and settle. GOBACK
GOBACK GOBACK FAREWELL LOCH THOM.

Kills me fairly and the weeping

WSGraham 4 12 75

*The annotated draft of 'Untidy Dreadful Table' represents the final draft of the poem;
the draft of 'Loch Thom' is only an intermediate draft. Both poems can be found in
W.S. Graham, New Collected Poems (Faber, 2004).*

[Late Between Disguises]

Make up your mind. Come in. You're lucky
To catch me here so late between
Disguises. I can see by your face
You are a mister of some importance

Or are you a Northern Earl? I said this
And he sat down and brushed the hail
Off his shoulders. We said nothing.
(Excuse me. May I look at what
I have put down. I want to make it
Right for you and your children running
Into the English language.) Anyhow,
This creature enters with epaulettes
Of hail and here we sit with no
Interpreter to change English
Into English. Too loud outside
To hear the Madron owl. I think
I see him going to speak. My cat
Not looking sees him almost beginning
To say something. What shall we do?

A typescript fragment with a single manuscript correction. Dated, in the author's
handwriting, 5 May 1973. W.S. Graham Estate archive.

FRAN LOCK

from *cordelia at the home for the incurables*

i

it has been said that i *suffer on purpose*; there is an art to that, and in an ugly soapstone vase the yellow rose aspires to texas not to sweetness. her fragrance is a craving you incline toward in vain. i swear i'm not *in love with pain*, but there is a splinter under my nail, and it is a piece of the *one true cross*. who has been bringing you flowers? and don't they know you cannot siphon life enough by suction through a cut? the rose is *trying* to grow, *trying* to stand on a snapped green tendon. oh, how sad. i crush her petals out of spite. we are alike. i also rush to water when i'm hurt. not to heal but borrow back forgetfulness, and every sink a sea in which my injuries are buoyed. if *love* becomes an unrecorded weight, there's joy in that, in going under, the way some bodies melt like floes of ice. a rose that cannot feed can only float. and you, some luscious drug has caught you in its velvety fatigue. the rose has put its yellow on like armour. a paper boat with its paraffin seal...

ii

how like yourself you are today, *not ill*, you said, but biologically beguiled. you've rolled around these pinkish-creamy walls for hours, like you are *the sound of the sea*. the hospice is mulling you over, concocts an *unconvincing illness* out of air. you *caught* this death, a salt wind under your sails. the water's meanest alibi. today your mind is cutlass-sharp and you could trim the white rind from a ten-foot wave. i didn't speak of *need* to you, or ask you if you'd ever loved a woman as the sea has loved: without fidelity or restraint. i did not ask you where you'd been or where you think you're going. yours is a sea of situations, not of places. *precision is the highest form of cruelty*. you speak of the land as a banishment. you have become prophetic. some depths cannot be reckoned: *some books are better drowned at birth...*

iii

the doctor was stripping the flesh from a long, thin phrase with yellowy incisors. my love is the disaster by which i will measure all future emergencies...

xiii

some memories can jar the spine like whiplash: a mobile goes off, spraying us in the face with its melodious ultimatum: *don't you want me, baby?* no, quite frankly. the air conditioning on, old ladies led about by their dainty sickness, mincing and shrieking in turns, in slippers; a fat one, baby-janing it outside the showers, popping her pout like a pressure sore. it's hot. i require coffee so black it sucks the colour from our surroundings. you're like a legionnaire crawling for water, holding out your arms. when i think about being here i realise i am *accustomed*, not *resigned*. i cannot cry, my eyes are dry enough to chip the glass of lesser marbles. i've been here before. its familiarity sits just the wrong side of contempt: chicory piss, the man in the next bed who is *so* fucking yellow, sat dead-centre like the hardest heel of cheese in a trap. the *sleepy heads* all welded to pillows, thin and flat as patties of meat. *empty heads*, unclassified conches through which the sea noodles again its contemptible eighties muzak. what? of course i'm angry! if i let myself love you, even for a moment, i'd come apart like a dirty snowball. resentment is the only thing that's holding me together. you should see it outside: unswappable wives with rocks sewn into their bellies like wolves; junkies conjuring dithery mischief from flailing sleeves, and a narrow dog, whining at a bus stop, enticed to shy allegiance by the crumbs in my jeans pocket. *things are tough all over, cupcake*, someone has graffitied on the wall outside of spar. the man obliviously bloking into his headset, the girl in impractical sandals, her pink feet cooked and trussed like meat on the bone. conjunctive lull of afternoon, a haze around the houses. the buses stink, inside and out. a boy with pushpin spots, his face an angry mass of geo-tags. today you were wide-eyed and roundly abusive, ahab on adrenaline. captain of the *absolute*, or *infinite*. you have the profile of some roman general, embossed against the light. conquest is a currency. the dying understand this. immortalise your sneer in gold upon an obol. or do not ask to be remembered, close your eyes...

xv

cry me a river. i couldn't come today. i couldn't make myself, i mean. i got pulled under a song and stayed in bed. i couldn't row myself to shore. now i'm getting coffee. girl i'm getting coffee from has an undelighted laugh. my last-ditch dirty jokes. her mouth is a blunt red pulse, wide and round with a new wound's promising succulence. i always liked to let my doom off its lead in a crowded room. i know that you do too. did. it's five o'clock, and the past tense is a *distinct* possibility. i want to run away forever, but i have no home to run from. i have £1.36 in change. there is no one to meet and nothing left to buy. there is no respite from the ethicless work of leaving, of being left. spineless ideation, and i said *every disappointment's like the first* – slurring fervour, squealing thrill – *like love*. and i said *i don't want to catastrophise...* but i do. i want the salty river's lick, a sleek limb in a silver gauntlet, carry me away, cry baby blue. i no longer expect better of people, have i said that already? i rage a lot. fathomless father, never one more worthy of the blame. i know you didn't ask for this, but i have clipped your silhouette and pasted it up among the stars on my ceiling between the bank robbers, squaddies, hunger artists. day by day your body looms, becomes ominous, prodigiously unappeased. i have been here before. and i understand mania's treacherous energy, how it is to be young, a stripling suitor to a living end you never bargained for, with all your brilliant schemes gone glittering up through a wet slit in your reason. once and future *enfant terrible* of the london underground, i know how it is to live by maladjusted tumult, black amusement, six a.m., when you cannot confront the former self you're shadow of. i wish that knowing knit things back together. as it is i'm slaking my slack mouth on prayer's brazen nectar. i think that pain might be your last great ostentation. playing the dane in a dunce's cap, a tricorne hat, half smiling. the moon is a tinfoil fascinator tonight, worn rakish in your honour. you are like the poor, you will always be with us. we resemble each other. you were a warrior, once, you'd grin and sink your teeth into any young and strutting error. my sorrow is a shore where things wash up. i wallow the received wisdom of the water, awaiting the change that is bound to come...

KIM HYESOON, *translated by Don Mee Choi*

A Face
Day Forty-three

World without a sound. Untouchable, flat world. When death dawns, world turns into a hard mirror. Faraway world of hope. The mirror reflects all things like the face of someone whose insides are dead. The shape of a woman appears in the mirror. Now you've become toeless feet. Now you've become fingerless hands. You've become a noseless, mouthless face. Your insides that are so far away yet close, the forest in your hair, light enters the rocky moon, and the sea wavers in your shoes. Birds fly up your sleeves and a horse weeps in your pants. The dissolving outline of a woman, a woman trapped inside a round mirror, a woman whose tongue is melting inside her mouth cries inside the slippery edge of the freezing mirror. The full moon wanes. Whenever the sleek mirror flashes flashes in her eyes, something heavy and transparent stomps on her face. The hard world can be seen but not entered, the world is white like a movie screen but with clenched fists. Perhaps the woman's faint arms are still stirring it.

A Doll
Day Forty-four

A doll watches another doll set on fire
watches it burn across the river then moves in closer
sees the scalp of the doll burning

Someone takes another someone away
Who put your doll on top of the woodpile?
Your body's all burnt up but you don't return
like a guest who asks to spend the night
then never wakes up

Who scoopscooped up and drank your mother's breast milk?
Who stole you and placed your doll in the stroller?
Who raised your clueless bones and sent them to school?

When you look at the photo of the outdoor cremation site in Varanasi, there's
perhaps a doll, perhaps a human, perhaps you, perhaps me, perhaps tears,
perhaps sweat, under a yellow blanket, a crushed thing stuck to the stretcher.

Underworld
Day Forty-five

The dead without faces

run out like patients

when the door of the intensive care unit opens

carrying pouches of heart, pouches of urine

The dead running toward the path of the underworld

turn into stone pillars when they look back and their eyes meet their past

The dead in their sacks look out with eyes brimbrimming with salt water

The dead become pillars of water as their tears melt their bones
The dead, gone forever, departed before you
pull amniotic sacs over their heads and get in line to be born again
and say that they need to learn their mother tongue all over again
that you're not there when they awake or even when they eat breakfast
When the dead swarmswarm down the mountain
like children who pour out of the door of the first-grade room
carrying their notebooks and shoe bags

a four-ton bronze bell with a thousand names of the dead engraved on it
        dangles from the helicopter
The helicopter flies over a tall mountain to hang the bell at a temple hidden
        deep in the mountains

Asphyxiation
Day Forty-six

Hence breath
Then breath
Next breath
Subsequent breath
Because breath
Such breath
And breath
Same breath
Thereafter breath
Thus breath
Always breath
Eventually breath
Perpetually breath
Yet breath
However breath
Therefore breath
In spite of breath
Breath till the bitter end

Death breathes and you dream but

it's time to remove the ventilator from death
it's time to shatter the dream with a hammer

Don't
Day Forty-nine

The warm buoyant breaths don't miss you
The winds that have left for reincarnation before you, that brush against the
    lips of your childhood don't miss you

The winter, the woman's ice heart, dead from sickness, drifting away in the
    infinite blue sky
with thin needles stuck all over it doesn't miss you

The leaves blow away, leaving their prints on the frozen river and

the one-hundred, two-hundred-story high buildings crumble all at once and

the spectacles with spectacles, shoes with shoes, lips with lips, eyebrows with
    eyebrows, footprints with footprints swept into a huge drawer don't miss you

The river is frozen eighty centimeters deep, a tank passes over it, and the fish
    beneath the ice don't miss you

The dog tied to the electric pole in front of the tobacco shop for fourteen years
    doesn't miss you

While the big wind takes away thousands of women dead from madness

the sound of the *yous* of your whole life, your hair falling

all of the winter landscape, wailing and wielding its whip doesn't miss you

Thousands, hundreds of thousands, millions of snow flurries don't miss you

Don't descend all over the world, howling, murmuring, searching for your
    snowman-like body buried in the snow, don't miss you and say I love you or
    whatever as if unfolding a beautifully folded letter

Don't miss you just because you're not you and I'm the one who's really you

Don't miss you as you write and write for forty-nine days with an inkless pen

JACK NICHOLLS

Auld Lang Syne

The year walks on his hands like a river, and the river is dirty
and it is tired, and it is stinking and it is grand.

And the river gambols clumsily into the party, a thin and noxious grappa.
The year is a river is a tumbler in a motley of grey, dirty grey, dirty

dark grey and dirty pale brown, stroking the keys of the baby grand
he dragged in with him, dampwarped and slimy – and he chants like a kappa,

dandles a boatskull and sucks at the ribs of a trolley. He spumes a dirty
laugh as he marches bailiffly round the party, trying to wring a grand

in kind from all present, for we owe him, we are all caught in his ceaseless oompah.
He clears his throat, declares: Bring me your freakshakes, your pulled pork and dirty

burgers, your every time he says "doomed" on *Grand
Designs* drink. I'll suck out your L-dopa

with a straw. You owe me. We mutter dirty
words half-heartedly, though make no grand

fuss, as we do indeed owe him. Bring me your spare five minutes. Your biccie and
   cuppa.
Your Friday drinks with the lads. Your flat white. Your half a glass with dinner. Your
   dirty

pint. The river is a year is an old man dressed as a fool and making a grand
sweep with his arms. We owe him everything, a total *mea culpa*.

The room fills with water, soddening the carpet, making the walls dirty.
We swirl toiletwise, curse his name, as if our deaths were significant, our
    icons grand,

our small splashed lungs much more than logged prepupa.
The laptop speakers gurgle out an underwater 'Dirrty'

and we spend our last molecules of oxygen enjoying a nostalgic boogie, a grand
R-rated gesture to the river, our wild bodies swollen with chutzpah,

some of us starting to float. This is typical: we have always made the water dirty,
we are expert flotsam. Through the filthy wobble the telly fireworks chime the
    grand

finale, midnight, and we gaze up at the river is a jester is a Sherpa,
high-up, unfollowable, and he clicks his heels and exits, his chore done, the
    dirty

dishes ignored, but pointedly. Those still breathing breathe, and the new year
    makes a grand
entrance, banging the French windows. He smiles, sweet as a grandpa.

We kiss each other and borrow his money. He pats our heads firmly, a nice
    new boss.
And hey, I can feel it, me and you, this is going to be our year, baby.

FIONA BENSON

Fly

Spring broke out but my soul did not.
It kept to sleet and inwards fog.
Forget-me-nots around the path,
a speckled thrush; I spoke rarely
and had a sour mouth. I couldn't make love.
My husband lay beside me in the dark.
I listened till he slept. I picked out
all the bad parts of my day like sore jewels
and polished them till they hurt.
I wanted to take myself off like a misshapen jumper,
a badly fitting frock. I wanted
to peel it off and burn it in the garden
with the rubbish, pushing it deep
into the fire with a fork. And what sliver
of my stripped and pelted soul there still remained,
I'd have it gone, smoked out, shunned,
fled not into the Milky Way,
that shining path of souls, but the in-between,
the nothing. But this overshoots the mark,
this gnashing sorrow, so Wagnerian;
it was more a vague, grey element I moved in
that kept me remote and slow,
like a bound and stifled fly, half-paralysed,
drugged dumb, its soft and intermittent buzz,
its torpid struggle in the spider's sick cocoon.
What now if I call on the sublime?
What bright angels of the pharmakon
will come now if I call and rip
this sticky gauze and tear me out?

Village

I walked up and up. Thought the same cracked thoughts
about the same cracked stuff: ego, work –
why hadn't I been published in this, invited to that,
yak yak yak, meanwhile shrapnel, exile,
the bombed, the drowned; tent cities that stretch for miles.
I left the kids yelling blue murder,
left them to their father, slammed the door, walked fast.
My halfway mark is a wind-pruned beech,
and its dipped illuminated leaf was twisting
like holy fire in the last rays of the sun
as its wheel slipped low over the horizon.
I already toiled in the lane-trough's early dusk,
for all the lanes are high-hedged here and thoroughfare
to the immortal geometries of flies, scribbling
their pentagrams and signs invisibly on air.
That beech was the last lit tree in the universe,
and it sang with a strange and lonely friction to the sun,
some *don't be gone*, some treaty for the dawn.
I walked up to the galvanised steel gate
and hoiked myself over and found myself watched
by a large buck rabbit drumming his foot
on the hard red dirt, a colony alert.
Here was the rapeseed in fluorescent bloom,
leguminous and sprung, its acid yellow lime
erupting into beauty. Always the urge
to lie down here and tryst, away from crowded rooms
and all their petty navigations; to lie down
headlong with my lover, to open for the deepest kiss.
The rabbit turned its long white scut
into the rapeseed's wiry wood and disappeared.
I trespassed the whole wild edge of the field
and found the farmer's timber stacked in long,

sawn cords, seasoning for next year's fires,
and in amongst it woodlice, their soft and huddled shells
a useless sort of shield, and milky spores of mould,
cantilevering the bark in secret, wood-dark coombs.
There's nowhere safe in the world for an exiled child.
I could see my village held in the crook of the valley
along the dwindled stream; the children
were simmering down, getting into bed;
the men were reading them stories, kissing their heads.
And I felt love for my small and human life down there,
its tenderness.

Hide and Seek

After her swim I wrap my child warm
and take her to the changing room
and lie her down to dry. She holds the corners
of the towel up over her face
like a soft, turquoise tent and yells
"Hide and seek! Hide and seek!"
I lift an edge and shout "Boo!"
and she shrieks with laughter –
I can feel the heat rising from her body
and smell the chlorine – she hides again,
and again I peek under and she's beside herself
with happiness – she's at an age where she thinks
that if she just stands still in the middle of the lawn
I will not see her, that somehow she is gone –
but always, in the pockets behind this game,
there is this residue, this constriction,
families squeezed behind false walls
or hidden under the floor. I think of the soldier

sensing the hollow under his sole
and prying up the board on all those cramped
and flinching humans; but mostly I think
of the mothers, their hearts jumping out of their mouths
trying to shush their children – my firstborn now,
who's never been able to do as she's told,
how she'd have writhed and screamed and bitten like a cat
if I'd tried to hold her quiet, how I'd have hurt her,
clamping her mouth, trying to keep her still.
The trapdoor is always opening, the women and children
are herded into the yard – and I ask myself if,
when my daughters were pulled from me,
I would fight and scream to keep them,
or let them go gently, knowing
there was nothing to be done?
If we were pushed into the showers
would I pretend it was only time to get them clean?
We are not meant to write of the Shoah,
we who were not there, but on bad days it's all I can think of,
the mothers trying to shield their children with their bodies
under the showers, screaming for mercy, begging for rain.
And it's never over – here are the children
riding to the border in fridges as the air becomes hot and thin,
their tiny bodies glowing like bright sardines
on the custom officer's hand-held scan;
and here is the tribesman carrying your husband's genitals
and a bloody machete, and you are a mother
running for your life with a baby tied to your back
and two children by the hand
but one small son is falling behind;
Jesus fucking Christ, I don't know who
I'm teaching you to hide from, but look
how eagerly you learn.

[Zeus] Anatomical Dolls

It's hard to explain. Let me show you
with the anatomical dolls. They have buttons for eyes
and details under their pants you wouldn't believe –
look underneath at the girl's folded labia, vagina,
the tucked-in silk-and-string umbilical
of a pull-down, poppet foetus, or the male's
miniature penis, his cotton-bag scrotum,
his sphincter ringed in little puckered stitches.
So the girl doll took off her frilly knickers
and the boy doll pushed down his trousers
and did this, and you might think it was love
if you hadn't seen Act One, the male doll
playing Punch, Judy trembling and bruised,
her bloody nose. Tell me what's the word for this,
this spreading of the legs and lips to delay violence,
and where's the rough music, all my charivari pots
and wooden spoons to out you Zeus,
to drive you through the streets, with songs
that find a name for you at last,
you filthy pimp, you animal, you rapist.

Haruspex

October and the blown
mushroom dissolves,
its volva clubbed,
its stalk and cap,
its singed and musky gills.

I've spent too long collapsed
over this inwards dark
disembowelled, gone
to ground, fingering
my own wet spills

and bodily secretions,
a dream in which
I am fucking and weeping –
my mind has been wrong
for a long long time.

Here is its fruit.
It's true,
I hear voices
and talk to myself.
I am done with shame.

HANNAH LOWE

Milked

When Christine speaks of Milton, blind, composing
his poem by night, and in the morning, waiting
for a scribe to 'milk' his words, I think of the week
I left you, darling – you were six months old –
to fly to Kuala Lumpur, my breasts engorged
for fourteen airborne hours, Simon waiting
at the gate, an hour's drive to his penthouse flat,
then finally, the guest room, a breast pump, relief.

Except the motorised suck is nothing like
a baby's skilful mouth, more like a message
to the breast that it should keep on making milk,
a charge the left one heard far louder than
the right, long days and nights of leak and thud
and quietening the nipples' dripping tap
with cubes of ice and sanitary pads.

Next door, Si had a local girl, three decades
younger and who, at his age, could refuse
the nimble body of a teenager?
Those evenings, while I siphoned in the darkness
and poured away my milk, they were naked
at the mirror – a blade, cocaine and chemical smoke.

That girl was territorial and scared
of me, and in my head I told her, look,
my left breast is a hedge-fund manager
with a pricey wife and kids at Charterhouse
whose epic fraud will soon be found; my right breast

is a train driver who hasn't slept in days
speeding down the track toward a chancy bend.

It was dawn when I came back, and climbed the stairs
to find you sleeping in our bed, your bottle

on the pillows, drained, your dad's exhausted face.
We had rats and climbing damp, and in my case,
six thousand pounds. It wasn't what you think.

I sat, took off my shirt, my soaking bra –
held you to my chest to make you drink.

Cold Stone

Outside Victoria Station, my mother trips and falls,
her glasses crashing to the cold stone
and for a moment she lies like a stunned child

thrown from a bike or scooter. And is she my child
now, my mother, now doctors and anger and falls
are much of her news, now her phone is a cold stone

nobody calls? Two strangers lift her from the stone,
the woman, her age, soothes me, makes me a child.
But every night since then, I dream my mother falls

again, again, again, glass to stone, my lonely child.

DOIREANN NÍ GHRÍOFA

Craquelure

At 5.56, some glitch, some distraction,
some finger twitch, slips the phone
from her grip and sends it smashing
into the pavement. We all flinch.

Soon, the bus jolts us through streets
and suburbs and into the dark.
Night makes a mirror of the window
and makes me a spy. I sit behind her and pry.

I watch her fingers slide over the fractured glass,
jabbing the lattice of cracks where the clock's
digits progress, still, splintered italics eclipsing
the child's smile, his face grown suddenly lined.

A little ink begins to leak from the rifts.
It grows dark. Oh, it grows dark and darker.
Take us back, driver.
Lurch this bus into reverse.

As a conservator rewinds lines
from a painting's tempera eyes,
bring us back. Let her lift her phone
from the path, unharmed.

Let her shiver, check the time,
sigh at the child's smile,
slide the phone back in her pocket,
its digits slipping to 5.59.

KATHRYN MARIS

The death of empiricism

When you think someone is a sadist, it may mean that you are a masochist.

You can never know if a photo of the president with a dog has been faked, whether in the Photoshop sense or the psychological sense.

If a spring flower blooms in December it may mean we are fucked but, equally, if a flower blooms in April we may be fucked in that instance too.

If Shakespeare wrote about a woman dressed as a man dressed as a woman dressed as a man, perhaps he wasn't considering gender at all.

Your fear of abandonment above every other condition may have emerged because you are a deserter.

Someone who makes the gestures of love may not love you, and someone who makes none of the gestures but behaves in a loving way also may not love you.

Difference is initially exciting, but ultimately more exciting is finding any thing in which you can see your self.

What looks like the flag of Japan may be a bloodied bedsheet; and an attempted mating call may rouse only those of the wrong sex.

Power is a superficial state, but a superficial state (e.g. one that erects empty villages) is not likely to be powerful, except when it possesses a hydrogen bomb.

Humility may seem like good medicine, but it makes the organism – and those organisms attached to it – weak.

The flip side of a close-knit family is an honour killing.

Someone who hisses when you offer her food is not the snake you want
in your house when the apocalypse comes.

That your daughter asks for a glass of milk while you are reading her
this poem does not mean it is without sustenance.

from *The House of Atreus*

Then we had the best meal of our stay

Clytemnestra

Then we had the best meal of our stay,
a place you could pass without noticing,
a small establishment with a single woman
serving a whole room of diners & I wept
as we ate, *I have felt so fretful for so*
many years, not believing I'm loved.
He countered with his own frustration:
our constitutional differences.
I tried again: *I want us to be*
a family or I'll go back to my
original one. When we left, the
proprietress kissed us on both cheeks.
[I'm constricted on this Eurostar,
two bags at my feet & suffering from wine.]

We had a big row yesterday

Iphigenia

We had a big row yesterday:
I was agitated because
he keeps mentioning the self-harm
in such a selfish way, as though
to slice up my veins was violent
to *him*. When I asked him to drop
it, he claimed I want to "control"
him. As I left, I shouted, *Why
can't we just be together?* He
said, *So I can live in this hell
all the time?* and I said *On the
contrary* [yes I used those words]
*don't you see I'm only like this
when you leave me, which is always.*

MANIFESTOS

In this series, we invite poets to write their own 'poetry manifesto'

. . .

Harmony Holiday
"Somebody who loves me"

I am inside somebody who loves me. I can't help but hear Whitney Houston's proclamation, *I wanna dance with somebody, with somebody who loves me* when I announce that, that's the pitch it accesses, and it's accurate, I want to take myself dancing and poetic language allows it, although the deliberate confession I launched into the dance with derives from a desire to revise or refuse the truth Amiri Baraka offered in his poem 'An Agony. As Now' when he wrote *I am inside someone / who hates me*. No. Not anymore. Not today. No more patient and methodical self-sabotage or effort to feel my way into brown skin with self-loathing as the neural-transmission. No more shrill militancy to protect us from our private sense of helpless sublimation. I am inside somebody who loves me. She would kill for me. She writes in order to avoid having to murder the ones who are inside somebody who hates them. As an act of love she addresses their pathology with reckless authority and most of all, movement, a way of penetrating space that refuses to close the self to the self, that is no longer complicit with being held hostage behind self-inflicted enemy lines. And she understands that her position is one of luxury, that being in a black body and loving it in the West is either a lie or insane or deranged or anti-social or so electric and full of life it nearly knocks you down as it passes through you as lucid resolve, redemptive and precarious.

From that loving pact, can a poem be choreographed or improvised the way a dance can? Maybe, if it can be inhabited the way a body is, if each word and phoneme indicates a part of a living system moving through space and time with immortal intentions, if the words populate a vision and also dangle that vision over the ledge of the unknown, testing and establishing its boundaries in the same gesture. If the poem is inside of a syntax that loves it, it cannot help but propel with the grace and rigor of a spinning body. But if I am inside somebody who loves me but I articulate that love in a language that denies me, that wants me to bend to its broke-down grammar, acquire the tension of its jittery stops and starts, a showdown is brewing, some kind of revenge for the haunt of false epiphanies and memories wilting in the shade of namelessness is on the horizon.

Somewhere between the somebody who loves me and the language that tries to exploit me for my ineffable vital energy, there's a crevice for intention/inevitable linguistic disobedience that thus obeys that love we begin with and occupy relentlessly, and there are poems lighting up that crevice and broadening it into sanctuary. The poems I love, and love to write, exact the joy of that space as retribution, reaching out with rage and tenderness for new utterance and ideas as well as for the ancient ones, on both sides casualties of colonialism, so that when we note that everywhere members of the African diaspora live, an unapologetic practice of improvisation and 'speaking in tongues' and dancing to go with it and religion to legalize it and jazz music to canonize it into something secular that the colonizer's mind can openly fetishize, we realize that we are witnessing a poetics of refusal so sophisticated it passes for something verging on the folkloric. The black and brown bodies of the world refuse to follow the drab codes of western language/logic, in thought or in form, and poetry is our most effective weapon and reprove besides our actual bodies. Though I'd rather not label it war. I'd rather say I am inside somebody who loves me and I can prove it by the way she speaks of me, to me, and through me, and by the rules she refuses to follow. In not so much a hierarchy as a system, the way we move through space and time, how we treat and see our bodies, how valuable we believe we are, how free, how eager to know ourselves and reflect that knowing as being, becomes the way we think and those thoughts become the way we live especially when surrendered beyond the stage of vibration into spoken language. The low self-esteem that blackness sometimes garners can be observed in our mimicry of the colonizer's languages and forms. As we move toward new and hybrid poetic textures that reflect the authentic rhythm of our thoughts and the highest potential of our actions and rituals, we will be moving away from somebody who hates us toward someone who loves us, is in love with us without the deranged blur of inverted rapture that would-be oppressors feel. And this love is our only duty, acting worthy of ourselves in that way is. So we write in our terrible and terrorizing and irresistible latinate or romance or patois languages, how we want to look and feel and sound and be, and that way if it's ugly everybody's to blame, and that way if it's beautiful we're orphans again, children of the sun again. Our poems are instructions in that way, and every colonized person is a poet as soon as she uses the language trying to break her in to rebuke and dismantle itself instead, to body itself, topple itself, knock that self over in loving disapproval of being muted by anyone. I crave poems like that and a world wherein they are eternally and eagerly welcomed and at last, demanded – mandated. You might be writing about three black laborers running through high grass to catch a rabbit but you also let them grab it by the neck and weep as it squeals and set it free and go hungry. Blackness defies western logic, so must the poems inside black bodies who love us enough to expose and know that ruthless interior. Migos' 'Walk It Talk It' is a good anthem for these methods. Hip-hop is way ahead of literature on the freedom train but we're busy hoppin' cars with anti-heroic love poems for cargo, busy barging in, busy being born, busy falling in love with ourselves again and again in the sensual blank of utter alienation, everything is familiar and ripe for our liberated forms. It's like the first time you catch a glimpse of yourself through eyes that notice and really believe, how beautiful you are, and the way that realization cannot be shut down by doubt or tentativeness ever again, and so must be lived, the poem is that moment of enchantment and its endlessly unruly future.

Wendy Cope
"Truth to feeling"

When I was asked to write this, one sentence came into my mind: "I give to the world what I have in my heart and that is the end of it." Franz Schubert. Since coming across that quotation I've felt that he speaks for me too.

There's another quotation that's important to me and it qualifies the above. This one is by T.S. Eliot. "The greatest difficulty for a poet is to distinguish between what one really feels and what one would like to feel." Those words are from an article about George Herbert. Eliot thought him "as sure, as habitually sure as any poet who has written in English" at avoiding "moments of falsity".

Moments of falsity ruin a poem. Or, to paraphrase Les Murray, "You can't poe a lie". He doesn't, of course, mean that a poem can't be a work of fiction. But truth to feeling matters in fiction as well. If Dickens hadn't really cared about the poor, his novels wouldn't be as good.

When a poet exaggerates or embellishes his or her feelings, the reader is alienated, not necessarily understanding why. I've read poems that leave me saying, "Oh, come on, pull the other one." Often such poems are implausibly and relentlessly high-minded. I don't think it's usually a question of deliberate untruth. It may be that the poet is out of touch with what he or she really feels. Or it may be a failure to find the right words to convey the truth with accuracy. That takes work and technical skill. The poet Rob Wells has something interesting to say on the subject in his interview with C.B. McCully in *The Poet's Voice and Craft* (1994). "I find it uncanny how, the more a poem seems to reduce itself to the mere resolution of a technical problem, the more unerringly it homes in on the truth I didn't know was there to tell." That's true for me too, and it is, indeed, uncanny.

When a poem isn't working I ask myself, "What is the truth of the matter?" and I try to pin it down more accurately. This process can be therapeutic. My view on writing poetry as therapy is that if it works as therapy it will work as poetry, and vice versa. I have sometimes begun working on a poem in a suicidal frame of mind and managed to work my way through to feeling less desperate. If the resulting poem seems to be a good one, I am cheered up quite a lot.

A poet is someone who enjoys playing with words. Playfulness is not in the least incompatible with saying something serious, important and/or deeply felt. One of the things I love about George Herbert is that you can see him having fun with the forms he uses, although all his poems are utterly serious reflections on his relationship with God. Some of my poems are merely playful and could justly be described as light verse. But not many of them.

One or two people who have been taught by me on Arvon courses have been pleasantly surprised to find that I didn't try to persuade everybody to write in traditional forms. I do know a few formalists who believe that all poems should make use of traditional metre. I don't agree with them. I enjoy traditional forms, both as a reader and as a writer, and that's why I use them a lot. I don't, as anyone who has read my poems will have noticed, use them all the time.

However, I am the kind of person who is inclined to look for the rules and obey them. It's an inclination I need to fight. Once, when I had written a poem with some foreign words in it, I said to James Fenton "I wasn't sure if we were allowed to use foreign words until I remembered that Eliot did it."

"Wendy," said James, speaking very slowly and emphatically, "We are allowed to do whatever we like."

Indeed we are. But there are a few things I wish people wouldn't do and I'll use the remaining space to mention one of them. In the last chapter of *The House at Pooh Corner*, Eeyore attempts to write a poem. He wants to say that all Christopher Robin's friends send him their love. I can't quote the poem because I tried that once before and the Milne estate wanted to charge me an arm and a leg. The point is that Eeyore struggles because he realises that "friends" and "send" don't rhyme. He alters "friends" to the singular. But then he has to put an 's' on "send". He sees that you can't rhyme "friends" with "send" or "friend" with "sends". Milne would never have done that, I wouldn't do that, and until recently nobody did it. But nowadays poets do it all the time. I call such rhymes "Eeyore rhymes". This is unfair on Eeyore who did at least understand that there was a problem.

Yes, we are allowed to do whatever we like. And I am allowed to disapprove.

Choman Hardi
"We will not be bystanders"

Poets write out of various needs and interests. For those of us who are interested in the intersection of literature with social justice, telling the truth becomes the driving force behind our writing, the reason we persevere. A Rwandan woman, in a conference about genocide and the arts, said it all when she stated: "I am not afraid of dying, I am afraid of not telling the truth." Some people argue that there is no 'one truth' but rather a multiplicity of 'truths'. They may ask, Whose truth are you writing about? My answer is simple: I write the truth of those whose suffering falls within the blind spot of mainstream consciousness, who are marginalised and silenced, unable to influence the discourses that inform the decisions affecting their lives.

Coming from a stateless and patriarchal community with a history of mass violence and repeated betrayal by those who had been counted as friends, I try to tell the stories of those who live through the reality of it, particularly the women. Mass violence and genocide leave communities saturated in grief, trapped in the graphic stories of violence, and bereft of means of healing. These stories multiply quickly, reproduced in daily conversations, in the media, and in the realistic and unimaginative artistic representations: the paintings full of skulls and soldiers' boots, plays full of roaring planes and falling victims, poetry that cannot rise above the simplified everyday rhetoric.

Unable to cope and desperately trying to move on, communities try to shut out those painful voices. Over time, the stories of survivors lose significance. They are ridiculed, doubted, and even turned into jokes. The disconnections and rupture caused by mass violence run deep. Individual survivors are victimised once again when, in the aftermath of the atrocities, they are stigmatised in their own communities, left behind, not heard, not believed, not understood. Some insist that their suffering "cannot be put into language". They feel that words fail to recount their experiences, can no longer communicate their pain, and lack the power to reconnect them to the communities from which they have become alienated.

At times like this, when the truth is muddled, confused, hidden, and gradually forgotten, when a story is too complicated, too painful, and too elusive to tell, poetry comes to our rescue. It provides that safe space in which to tell those stories. Poetry is not about facts, which interest courts and historians, it is about the truth. In a poem, factual details may or may not be present: what matters is the meaning of the event. Good poetry of witness can enrich our understanding of humanity, tell the truth in its full complexity, highlight the failure of conventional morality at desperate times, show how violence disconnects people and destroys normality and domesticity, and generally address the grey areas that we avoid in our everyday lives.

This kind of poetry requires immersion in the experiences and stories of those who suffer. It requires living with the details and knowing that contradictions and inconsistencies are inherent in any narration. We need to research the topic thoroughly, listen with all our might, and allow ourselves to be vulnerable.

At a very difficult time in my life, when I was grappling with secondary traumatisation associated with taking on others' suffering, a man told me, "You don't have to experience pain in order to understand it." He was a massage therapist and he spoke like a good and rational scientist. Of course he could not feel my pain – how it was distributed through my organs and muscles, how it disrupted the rhythm of my hormones, how it slipped into my unconscious and resurfaced in my nightmares – but he was able to help me heal through understanding my pain.

What he told me made perfect sense, and helped me gradually get back on my feet and focus on completing my academic book on the subject. But I now know that good poetry of witness comes from that soreness, from feeling outrage and fear, from that place where we are bewildered and we feel too much. Poetry is not science. We cannot speak the truth about suffering in poetry when we haven't emotionally experienced it. Understanding alone does not help convey the emotional tone of desperation, and it does not help rebuild the connections that have been severed by victimisation. So yes, we need to be willing to suffer, to share pain, to feel strongly. But this does not mean that our poetry should be 'emotional'.

There is a difference between emotional poetry and poetry informed by emotions. The stories we want to tell are already full of force, pain, and strong feelings, and we do not need to add another layer of emotion by adding our own. We need to hold back our anger and pain and let those stories speak for themselves. We must communicate the truth without alienating the readers and shouting in their faces, without being self-righteous and making them want to shut us out. We are trying to make comprehensible that which seems incomprehensible, to rebuild connections and facilitate understanding and empathy.

The key is to not release those poems too quickly but to live with them, mull them over. We may end up editing and re-editing for a long time. Each time, after we make changes, we must put the poems away for a while and come back to them with fresh eyes and ears. We may read them aloud, record them if we need to, and listen to ourselves reading them. We must take every word seriously, be aware of its nuances and undertones, question its place, its necessity. We must stay loyal to the truth without overwhelming the reader with too much detail, stay loyal to the person's voice and maintain her style of telling the story as much as we can.

One last thing: we shouldn't worry too much about negative criticism. There will always be people who will not appreciate our poetry. Some will say that this is not poetry's duty or role. Others will find it too traumatic and won't want to read it. Still others may argue that the poems themselves are not good, that they only seem good by virtue of their subject matter. The latter will hurt but the response is pretty simple. There is plenty of bad poetry about war, violence, poverty, and stigma. Subject matter on its own cannot make a poem serious and good. More importantly, one cannot separate subject matter from form in such a straightforward manner. If a poem speaks to others, if it conveys the voices it represents, and builds the connections we desire, then it works as a whole, not in part.

Ultimately we try to do our best as poets and citizens who have a responsibility towards others. We will not be bystanders. We will not be silent. We will expose the injustice inherent in the status quo and challenge the powerful. We will sing. We will shout. We will write good poetry. We will not die before telling the truth.

Prose from Poetry

FROM PAUL CELAN'S 'MICROLITHS'

Translated from the German by Pierre Joris

Aesthetics thus demands hiddenness and rewards it, ethics demands disclosure and punishes hiddenness

•

True poetry is antibiographical. The poet's homeland is his poem and changes from one poem to the next. The distances are the old, eternal ones: infinite like the cosmos, in which each poem attempts to assert itself as a – minuscule – star. Infinite also like the distance between one's I and one's You: from both sides, from both poles the bridge is built: in the middle, halfway, where the carrier pylon is expected, from above or from below, there is the place of the poem. From above: invisible and uncertain. From below: from the abyss of hope for the distant, the future-distant kin.

•

Poems are paradoxes. Paradoxical is the rhyme, that gathers sense and sense, sense and countersense: a chance meeting at a place in language-time nobody can foresee, it lets this word coincide with that other one – for how long? For a limited time: the poet, who wants to stay true to that principle of freedom that announces itself in the rhyme, now has to turn his back to the rhyme. Away from the border – or across it, off into the borderless!

·

'Automatic' poetry: unconscious, and it too thus reminiscence – and thus why not quote the brought-along, impregnated as it is with the spiritual, and therefore also points more clearly towards the spiritual. –

·

Process, *event* in the poem

descriptions – static
hence no actual 'theme' possible.

·

prose line to the end
poem line –
the omitted
man remains an interlocutor though you have to know how to captivate him

if from naturalism or through it there is a way to lyric poetry –
torn-offness

Not Rilkean enjambment!!

He who catching his breath between two lines of poetry looks around for comma or conjunction, misses out.

·

Re-membering
also pre-membering, pre-thinking and storing of what could be

Yeats: I certainly owe more to that poet than to Fr. surreal.

Strange. In front of a candle
Now I tried to render visible the grain of sand (Buber, Chass. – //
Nibelungens[on]g) that had to have been sunk into me too at some time.

Mother, candles, sabbath
But the poem led me out of this idea, *across* to a new level with this idea

·

It is part of poetry's essential features that it releases the poet, its crown witness and confidant, from their shared knowledge once it has taken on form. (If it were different, there would barely be a poet who could take on the responsibility of having written more than one poem.)

·

– Poetry as event
Event = truth ('unhiddenness', worked, fought for unhiddenness)
Poetry as risk
     Creation = / power-activity / *Gewalt-tatigkeit* (Heidegger)
Truth ≠ accuracy (-i-: consistency)

·

Endnote: Poetry 'a shrine with no temple'
                  <Heidegger: Hölderlin>

·

-i-
It belongs to the poem's essence, that it will release the author, the confidant from its confidence. If it were different, no poet would write more than one poem.

·

-i-
The conjunction of the words in the poem: not only a conjunction, also a confrontation. Also a toward-each-other and an away-from-each-other. Encounter, dissent, and leave-taking all in one.

·

-i- *Receptivity* as core attitude when writing poetry –

·

Poetry doesn't stand so much in a relation to time, but to a given *world era* –

·

– in each first word of a poem the whole of language gathers itself
– handiwork: hand / think through connections
            such as 'hand and heart'
            handiwork – heartwork

Beginning: 'Poetry as handiwork'? The handmade crafting of poetry?

Does making poetry have any kind of duration? And in what relation to time, to one's lifetime does such duration stand?

Recollection: How I *recited* the first poems (Schiller)

Receptivity

                              •

-i-   from the experiences of the author

The word in the poem is only partially occupied by experience; another part the poem occupies with experiences; a further part remains free, i.e. *occupiable*

                              •

Poetry and the poet's craft: two realms, I believe, different from each other, even though bordering on each other, and of which the second can be considered as the foothills of the first. Because the poem can never be the result of the mastery of the given poet, no matter how great and proven this mastery may be. The idea that the poet is before all a master of his language, may come closest to the reality of the poetic, while only laying open one of the access points. Because the language of poetry is also always already the other language, the first word of which pulls the poet into a new language-occurrence, to which he entrusts himself more or less unconsciously. Even the most intense introspection does not permit a remainderless overview of this occurrence – and thus puts the concept of overviewable experiences into question. Possibly in such a way that the poem puts up with the shared cognizance of the one who 'produces' it only as long as is necessary for its coming into existence. For each poem necessarily claims uniqueness, unrepeatability; in each poem reality is checkmated once and for all, the whole of reality is constricted to a hand's width of earth, and in this – royal! – constriction that is not only of space but also of time, it is given the chance to assert itself in the face-to-face with the poetic word (in which moreover all of language, i.e. language as possibility and as questionability, is simultaneously contained). No poet who would not again be released from this uniqueness would ever dare to write a second poem.

•

Poetry: Incursions of language into the daily.
    In our polychrome, not colour-happy dailiness,
    the language of the poem, if it wants to remain the language of
    the p., will by necessity be *gray*.

•

Thank and think have the same origin.

•

Because to speak, to speak like one's mother, means to dwell, even there where there are no tents.

•

Poems are porous constructs: here life flows and seeps in and out, incalculably strong-headed, recognizable and in the most foreign shape.

•

While translating: the capitulation of the 'counter-text'

•

The poem is monotone 'Nobody becomes what he is not'

•

Representativeness, of whatever order, I cannot arrogate for myself; I am a Jew and a German-language author.
    But experience and, from afar, fate, together with a need for responsibility and solidarity, are what guide this pen

•

Poésie, affaire d'abîme / Poetry, a matter of the abyss
    – 12.21.66.

•

La poésie déjoue l'image / Poetry foils the image

•

The poet: always *in partibus infidelium*

•

I do not speak of the 'modern' poem, I speak of the poem *today*. And to the essential aspects of this today – *my* today, for I do speak on my own behalf – belongs its lack of a future: I cannot keep from you that I do not know how to answer the question toward which morrow the poem is moving; if the poem borders on such a morrow, then it possesses darkness. The poem's hour of birth, ladies and gentlemen, lies in darkness. Some claim to know that it is the darkness just before dawn; I do not share this assumption.

CAROLYN JESS-COOKE

We Have to Leave the Earth Because We Know So Much

He buried the letter in a forest near Auschwitz
where it hibernated for forty winters,
ampersands of his hand dormant
as field mice, and for all   he knew
the letter would never be found, snows
might drink the ink or the ground
swallow it as a grave. But
                      the urge to bear
witness moved him past consequence
of being found to speak of what   he said
to those he led to the gas chambers –
that they were not here to be bathed
as they'd   been told.
           We are still in that place,
being moved past consequence or to death, or
to witness the taking of what is not owed.
We have not passed the urge to   obliterate
the Other. We have to leave the earth
because we know too many ways   to destroy
her, we have to write these things
we have to tell them to the forest
and the watchful snows.

MONA ARSHI

Like the first morning

I sit at the kitchen table where
the light is best, where the light is.
As mute as dawn, I blink her out,
examine her hands, ink-stained
and cold, her neck creaking like an
iron hinge cooling on a gate.
I search the patchpockets of
her dress, full of tiny perforated
shells and small yolk-coloured flowers
ruining the lining and I run my fingers along
her back and through her hair which flows
like lava across her pale collarbones.
When I flinch, she flinches, this
soft girl, this churning broken song.

Ghazal: Darkness

Around the base of the trees amongst the broad oaks
    I leave my daughters to ripen in the darkness.

Beneath the cunning soil's breath, sweet white snowdrops,
    their strewn hearts are glowing in the darkness.

The soil thanks us, we roll up our cuffs,
    fill our pocket mouths defenceless in the darkness.

A gentle murmured refrain like old rain,
    like snowflakes again we answer to the darkness.

I've seen those girls foraging for wild mushrooms,
    the rim around their retinas turning in the darkness.

We plant cloves – tiny armless gods into the loam,
    poke them deeper into the uncertainty of darkness.

My girls are distracted and starved of light,
    which is normal, which is essence of girl-darkness.

I slip outside and light a candle, cauterise a bud,
    Shabash I call to my girls – my praise in the darkness.

JACK UNDERWOOD

There Is A Supermassive Black Hole 400 Million Times The Mass Of The Sun At The Centre Of Our Galaxy And You Are Pregnant With Our Daughter

We are not unique, and we are.
Every galaxy has its warden.

Another fact is that the human mind
is not an all-purpose-device.
It is natural to be overwhelmed.
Sometimes the summer needs a snow-day.
The story of the mind is that we woke up
in caves and arranged the rocks to make
these intersections, and subsequent minor-
league fixtures; now we have intimate
waxing salons, overage, offshore, diffidence,
failed special handshakes in the lobbies
of the pyramids, songs always in the charts,
you look different tra-la have you done
something different to your self today?

The garden is crying, and I truly feel the mind
is not an all-purpose-device.
Sometimes the sky needs its tattered flag.
It is natural to experience things as difficult.

The story of difficulty goes that it
was experienced, then spread across
the land like a more efficient language,
like a wet kind of money in love.
It's natural to be overwhelmed.
Love can be both the train and the silence
that follows it down the track.

The garden will stop eventually.
Meanwhile traffic remembers and forgets itself
on the road beyond the window.
I am so scared, aren't you?
There is a supermassive black hole 400 million times
the mass of our sun at the centre of our galaxy
and she already responds to our voices.

A girl or woman in relation to either or both of her parents

also noun meaning weather as in I expect the good daughter
won't last or the daughter is expected to improve at the weekend
also verb meaning to be suddenly aware of overwhelming scale
as in we were daughtered by the magnitude of the cave system
and how well-preserved the paintings were or adj. meaning robust
as in such behaviour was met with a daughter response also noun
meaning overseer as in a daughter was assigned by the company
to assess whose work had been completed satisfactorily also noun
meaning metal jug for outdoor use as in we arrived at the shed
and the daughter was already full of autumn also noun meaning
a situation that forces the mind to conceive of the impossible
as in suddenly we had a daughter and it began to rain indoors.

RUTH McILROY

Change of Shift at the University Swimming Pool

The fact that suddenly as if he were in a chamber
and it was something like roofless
and his face was expressionless,
my swimming pool attendant, pool attendant
dumped his bag upon the table,
and if there could have been music
it would have been something deep and opening,
and I swam in the sacred lane for medium swimmers
barely knowing clockwise from anti-clock,

and he would put himself down as a cipher
in so far as this was none of his doing,
this twisting in on itself shedding strangeness
and I swam in a sacred hall partaking of sacredness.

For example I was in the sea at 4 a.m. today

and not one of the best parts of the sea around Southampton
I was under an oil refinery and the flame

it was opened in me that
I was not in the state to finding your voice
what a lot of things it exceeded to

a self collection occurred
lively but calmer I was out of available
satisfied of what sensations I tried

and everyone jumps into the turned-out-safe
that is stayedness and off you go we turned to me saying

PHILIP GROSS

Himself

A small bull,
squat and ginger, in a field
under fells – on the tourist route; maybe
that's what leaves him looking vaguely shamed

but still considerable,
a blunt bull, so unmoving
it's a violence almost to the eye: himself
cast in bronze, on the plinth of, commissioned by

who but himself
while round the moister
corners of the field cows move,
and heifers, slightly, constantly, cropping, at cud.

He's as still
as something that resists
comparison; any likeness, even
to (especially) another bull inflames him; he

might have to kill.
For now, though, he's rapt
in the fact of himself. His bulldom.
It's a poser. Does the lank long dangle of his prong

explain him: the will
rebooting, maybe, the old life-
and-death and for-a-living, chug-chug-
idling libido? Or cornered, in the midfield of his life

that's suddenly an edge,
the rest dropped into precipice,

most of Cumbria with it, into rising mist,
the cough-slip of the scree an echo's length below –

nothing else for it now but to stand
his small ground. Or he's gone
beyond that, saint

of bullhood, deep
in contemplation.

He could be praying for us.

The Age of Electricity

Already we're those creatures our grandparents would not recognise – the
children of electric light,
                              of nights on the town, of the thousand-bulb
fairground waltzer, waterfalls of neon up which appetite thrashes to mate.

   How many of us were conceived not in the tactful dark, but... hey,
   leave the light on – born a bit more knowing, just because of that?

Don't you feel it fizzing in your chromosomes, those tweaks of the helix,
filaments of what a darker age called fate?
                                             Or see its blips on the cortex,
eyes closed, blindfold even, sparks like static prickling your inside night?

   No escape from it now, not even if a sneeze of solar plasma ripped
   our grids and stamped the grand marquees of glow above our cities
   flat;

our bodies won't forget. Age ten, dared to it,

I lick-tipped my torch battery
terminals; it's still there, the squirm of small volts on my tongue, fizzle-
sweet

like dangerous sherbet. Or, age five, marooned by lights-out,
whimpering: I'd forgotten how to sleep. At last, my mother took me
out to meet

midnight in person. Streetlights staggered off to on, red/orange, as they
saw us, pavements shivering awake. What

kept her walking, the two of us
walking, me almost asleep and still walking, beyond our own or any street

I knew, I couldn't say. I huddled close in the long-ago-mothbally
dream of her beaver-lamb coat

that smelt how forever might smell. It felt right,

to be walking, on, on to
the horizons of ourselves and beyond, out of sight.

REBECCA GOSS

Reverse Charge Call

What we girls knew of emergency was slight but peril was waiting. Brown Owl led us to a strip of telephone boxes to demonstrate her wiseness, and the art of a reverse charge call. Redirected to our mothers in that practice run, we offered up the digits learnt for the task – operator confirming connection – our rescue by vibration and wire. The double rings released from that GPO rotary dial, my mother's thirty-year-old hand lifting its curve from the cradle, the syllables of my name falling against her face. I can't recollect a conversation. Doubt there was given time. But *What If* that call had been redirected to my grown-up self? The operator asking me to accept the sound of me, stood on a pavement in Essex in the 1980s, striving for a badge for my mother to sew to my sleeve. I'd be holding the receiver, decades ahead, proficient in hurt and living, hanging on to my girl-voice, unsure whether to take this one chance and hurl warning.

ALISON BRACKENBURY

Wednesday on the 97

Like family you complain about but love,
I am at home with buses. This is prompt.
At every stop it dawdles in the sun.

I do not phone, read, talk. I simply sit.
I watch deep sycamores dip to the south
as if the whole day is a cat that purrs
and I the tongue, vibrating in its mouth.

Sheela na gig, St Michael's, Oxford

Her legs are parted to the day.
They prised her from the tower wall
before car fumes ate her away.

She shows no face. She bears no breast.
The priests claim she is not obscene:
a builder's warning against lust.

I laugh. I brush them off. I stare
into the black line of her slit.
How deep lips dance, how bare, how bare.

Directions

(as given by Jenny Joseph, 2008)

"These maps will not help,"
I fan three, starred with ink.
So you bristle truth
As a cattle fence, wreathed with stiff wire.

"Do not turn off here!"
But you list every sign:
"Beds, Sofas, Sale." What shall we talk of,
Sofa or bed? You can flow on for hours.

"Look left. Watch for cars
Sweeping up Brimscombe Hill,"
Your bath is scrubbed white.
Pumpkins swell watered leaf,

"There are dozens of ways
Over Rodborough Hill."
Why did you leave London?
Who do you love?

"The cows walk straight at you,"
Your cellar is damp.
Letters lap you, like leaves:
I do not know your dark.

"Turn right, by Tom Long's Post,
Immediately left,"
You are wise as the mist.
I am not worth your shoe.

"You are in Windmill Road,"
You wait, twenty years on,
With your bent hips, sharp eyes,
Firm with children, your gate.
I shall follow your maps
For each twist of the road.
I am your good pupil,
I shall be late.

LAWRENCE SAIL

Birdcall
Remembering Helen Dunmore

Eight days on, in the morning dusk
of four o'clock, the summons
of the blackbird's liquid song
loops up from the garden
three floors below

It conjures the image of you looking out
from your own tall house, delighted
at the bird's-eye view across
the river and the city backed
by marching hills

Most of all, the river's coming
and going, with its endless traffic
of boats, its swarm of detail,
and the changes of light dinting
the surface with dazzle

...And the image of the bird itself, close
to our freckled foxgloves or the gatepost,
black plumage offset
by its crocus-yellow bill
and enquiring eye

How you cherished the world! And I see,
when abruptly the song stops,
how the bird has been calling
attention not to itself,
but the silence following

IGOR KLIKOVAC, *translated by the author and John McAuliffe*

Jovo

No one, they say, throws
a surprise like death, and,
the family that we were,
I immediately think
of a cheat of sorts, our
grand-uncle Jovo, whose
first wife, along with the flat,
got repossessed in the war
by a local Nazi. Afterwards,
he chewed the soft and
the hard of life, always lugging
the same look, infinite
surprise, easy to mistake
for ebullience or lunacy.
Once, when I was ill,
by way of encouragement,
he told me that death is merely
a theft, a brazen operation
that, fortunately, occurs only
once in a lifetime, though –
a wink – not necessarily
at the end...

RUTH PADEL

Clast

    When your mother dies
there's no one left to hold the sky.
    When I was small
    we lived on the top floor
in Wimpole Street   an attic window
looking out on a forest canopy of silver tiles
    where an owl
roosted in a revolving flue
after a long night's hunting in Hyde Park.
    When the wind blew
my mother held me up
to see the vent swing its cowl
    like a periscope
and two dark eyes appeared
looking back at us
from a nimbus of pale feathers.
    Face of a secret moon.

     •

In the last week
when we were all

        cancelling meetings
        making long-distance phone calls wherever we could
                    find a signal

        gathering over scratch meals
        running out of milk

that moment when true feelings light up suddenly
out of the square-cut stone of the everyday
and urgency swings in like a wrecking ball

one of my brothers said
that her twenty-first birthday   fell
during the London blitz.

Rainy September.
  Her brothers all away
                working in hospitals
                        submarines
                                labs in America

she was alone   with her disabled
older sister and their parents.
None of them remembered   until supper
                                when her mother
                                went upstairs
and came back with a ring.

I don't like to think of this.
No one excited for her
  as her brothers might have been
only something quick-found   that would do

in the blackout   autumn rain
            twenty miles from fires
      shaking   thunder on the night horizon.

That ring
      a piece of stuck-together love and hurt
splintered   by the invading shale or schist
                        of loneliness

I never heard of it till now
never saw it on her finger. Will we find it in
the small bashed-up brown case

of jewellery she never wore
we lugged to those valuers
for probate

or was it got rid of   lost
   given away
through the years that came after?

How do you prove
   and what can you value
under the mountain range

of the unconscious?
   We never ask
the bedrock question till too late.

ANTHONY ANAXAGOROU

After the Formalities

*In 1481 the word 'race' first appears in Jacques de Brézé's
poem 'The Hunt'. De Brézé uses the word to distinguish
between different groups of dogs.*

In that hard year grandparents arrived on a boat
with a war behind them and a set of dog leads.
Bullet holes in the sofa. Burst pillows. Split rabbits.
Passports bound in fresh newspapers. Bomber planes.
A dissenting priest. A moneybag sucking worry.
On the boat grandmother anticipated England's
winters with the others. Black snow on gold streets.
Grandfather grieved two dogs he'd left. Pedigrees.
Bluebottles decaying at the base of their bowls. The dogs
of England were different. The water though. Fine to drink.

*In 1606 French diplomat Jean Nicot added the word 'race'
to the dictionary drawing distinctions between different
groups of people. Nicotine is named after him.*

In London grandparents lived with only a radio.
A lamp favouring the wall's best side. Curtains drawn
round. Byzantine icons placed on paraffin heaters.
Arguing through whispers. Not wanting to expose tongues.
Stories circulating. What neighbours do if they catch you saying
"I'm afraid" in a language that sounds like charred furniture
being dragged across a copper floor. Grandfather. Always.
Blew smoke out the lip of his window. So too did his neighbour.
Colourless plumes merging amorphous. The way it's impossible
to discern the brand of cigarette a single pile of ash derives from.

*In his 1684 essay 'A New Division of the Earth' French physician
François Bernier became the first popular classifier to put
all humans into races using phenotypic characteristics.*

Mother's skin is the colour of vacations.
Her hair bare-foot black. An island's only runway.
Reports of racist attacks. Father turns up the volume.
Turns us down. Chews his pork. Stings the taste with beer.
Tells mother to pass the pepper. There is never a please.
He asks if she remembers the attack. The hospital. His nose.
A Coca-Cola bottle picked from his skull. Yes. She mutters.
The chase. Dirty bitch. How we'll make you White.
Aphrodite hard. Dirty dog trembling with the street light.
Please God. Not tonight. The kids.

In 1775 J.F. Blumenbach claimed in his seminal essay
'On the Natural Variety of Mankind' that it was environment,
not separate creations, which caused the variety in humans.

In the bathroom mirror I spat blood from my mouth.
Quaver breath and suburban. My brother desperate to piss.
Pulled the door open. Asking. What happened?
I tried to fight and lost? Why? Because the island
we come from is smaller than this. Their names are shorter.
Pronounceable so they exist. Even after their noses break
they still don't hook like ours. Their sun is only half peeled.
He lifted his top to show me two bruises. To remind me
of something. How history found its own way of surviving.
A dark wash mixed with the whites spinning round and around.

In the bathroom mirror my brother spat blood
from his mouth. Souvla breath and home. Me.
Desperate to piss. Pulling the door open. Asking.
What happened? He tried to fight and lost? Why?
Because the island we come from is larger than this.
Here. We chew up too much of their language.
Leave behind an alphabet of bones. We will never exist
in their love songs. How many bruises does it take

to make a single body? I left him. Surviving history.
A dark wash mixed with the whites spinning round and around.

In 1859 British naturalist Charles Darwin wrote
On the Origin of Species by Means of Natural Selection,
or the Preservation of Favoured Races in the Struggle for Life.

If the house phone rings after midnight someone
you know is dying. Breathing in ten black moons
under a siren or belfry. From the wound in my uncle's
back leaked the first atlas. Blood escaping him
like a phantom vaulting over the spiked gates of heaven.
The knife. Half steel half drunk. The motive. Skin or prayer.
We went to visit. In the window's condensation his daughter
wrote *Daddy Don't Die*. On the water of her breath.
That evening my father came home. One hand trumpet.
The other wreath. All his fists the law.

In 1911 eugenicist Charles Davenport wrote in his seminal book,
Heredity in Relation to Eugenics, *"Two imbecile parents,*
whether related or not, have only imbecile offspring".

She had the same colour hair as Jesus. Most boys smile
after. When we were done I moved a blonde streak
from my arm wondering how much of my body
was still mine. I smelt of rain atop an old umbrella.
My fingers a burnt factory. She asked if I was her first
and when I said yes she smiled. Pulling the covers up
whispering not to get too comfortable. How her father
would be back. The bed now a continent. The duvet
locking me to its borders. On the shelf a gollywog
above her family portrait. Poised like a saint.

The 1943 famine of Bengal killed 4 million people. Churchill
ordered food to be sent directly to British soldiers in Europe. On hearing
the number of Bengalis who'd perished he asked, "Why hasn't Gandhi died yet?"

Outside the KFC racists have always looked
so sure to me. Like weathermen. Like fact.
Driving his skull into mine like a belief. I saw
how even evil can feel warm and smell good
when close enough. A crowbar. Wedged against
my throat. Slowly the lights began to wave. Chips
by my feet. Black iron warming my skin so silently
I could hear how suffering learns to soothe the jaws
of antiquity. These men. Irrational as any God. And me.
Emptying inside the promise of my oxygen tank.

"Those whom the gods wish to destroy, they first make mad.
We must be mad, literally mad, as a nation to be permitting
the annual inflow of some 50,000 dependants, who are
for the most part the material of the future growth
of the immigrant-descended population." – Enoch Powell, 1968.

After the formalities of course I said London
and of course he asked again. When I said Cyprus
he leaned into his chair recalling a family holiday.
The weather sublime. The people accommodating.
Particularly towards the English. How it was a shame
about the Turkish thing. And your parents. When did they enter
here? In the late '50s I replied. So before the Immigrants Act?
Yes I said. Before. Well good for them. He said.
Putting the lid on his pen. Closing his pad.
Asking me to talk a bit more about my previous roles.

In 2001 philosopher Robert Bernasconi wrote
"The construct of race was a way for white people to define
those who they regarded as other."

In those days I was required to fill out forms
with multiple boxes. Some I left blank. My father
would notice my omission. Filling in the white
option with his black biro. I crossed it out.
Telling him I'm going with 'other'. My mother
wearing the same sad skin as before said we are not
White. The look he gave her was. Snatching the form
from me. The same X dominating so much White.
Let me tell you. Nobody in their right mind need
make themselves such an obvious target. He affirmed.

"It's amazing how ideas start out, isn't it?" – Nigel Farage, 2016.

My grandmother will die. Somewhere in her skeleton.
White sheeted. Iodoform thick. Her mouth all beetle.
My family will gather round her body. All fig. My mother
will look for coins. Despite there being nothing for money
to save. Another lady. Dying the same. Will goad our kind.
Through thick tubes she'll scorn. Her voice. A bluebottle's
hot wings. You're all dogs. Foreigners. And dirty. Outnumber us
even in dying. The nurse will apologise for the whole of history.
Drawing the curtain. Mud is always the last thing to be thrown.
A prayer reaching for the pride of an olive. Like a hint. To hold.

Essay

I KNOW THAT MEN CAN MISTAKE

Tom Paulin's Love's Bonfire, *the dash and poetic authority*

Andrew McMillan

One of the things I've always been interested in, in relation to poetry, is the idea of working towards the truth. I don't mean telling the "what-actually-happened truth", as the great Irish poet Rita Ann Higgins has called it, but rather the creation of art that moves towards the 'poetic truth', that which gets to the root of a particular feeling, incident, or moment in time, in ways that might be almost entirely fabricated. Truth, then, as a synonym for honesty: how we honestly live in the world, even if we have to make things up to show that.

Poets will often find themselves in rooms with people who want to write; who are oftentimes wondering how they might make their work more 'truthful'. After talking of sincerity, or plainness in a poem, my own workshops will tend to move on to an idea of indecision in the voice of the poem's persona (which Jack Underwood's essay in the previous issue of this magazine distinguished from a "philosophical, empathetic" state of being uncertain). I've found myself, over the years, constantly returning to the poems in Tom Paulin's *Love's Bonfire* (2012). The collection features several poems which are expert in destabilising the authority of the poem's voice; rather than being told what something is in a sure declarative, the reader is given a set of potential options, or is given something with one hand only to have it taken away by self-correction with the other. Paulin uses the dash, that grammatical shorthand for something perhaps slightly less formal, to achieve this effect.

Take the opening of 'A Spruce New Colour' for example:

> It all depends on your point of view
> but from mine – and I know that men
> can mistake colours and shades
> – from mine the new suspen-
> sion bridge at Toome is puce
> – puce or maybe lavender –

All twenty-six lines of the poem carry on like this, oscillating between different points of view and different opinions. The only sure moment or definite image the poem is able to offer up is "the police station / built like a barracks behind high walls" – we'll come back to that line later. In workshops this is a great poem for discussing that idea of 'poetic truth' – because what is the human condition if it's never to be certain, to always second guess and to always reconsider what it is we've just said? The fact that Paulin can achieve this with just a little punctuation has always fascinated me.

How should we term these self-intrusions into the poetic line? I was not, for the longest time, sure; I abandoned the fixed position and certain voice of the 'critic'. I quite liked 'in-step', with its suggestion of coming out of the line and stepping into a new tangent of thought, but I've ultimately settled on the more mundane and literal 'dash'. Its evocation of striking or flinging something with great force also seems appropriate. Particularly in his later poems, it feels as though this is what Paulin is doing: quickly shifting the focus of a line or flinging the idea back to the reader – giving them the authoritative position, and asking them to make up their own mind.

This dash isn't something one sees much of in Paulin's very early work. In his debut collection *A State of Justice* (1977), the alternating indented line is favoured as way of bringing the undulating rhythm of the landscape into the poems. In 'Under a Roof', from this first collection, the dash towards the end of the second stanza simply adds further detail to the description, albeit with slightly more force than previous lines, rather than redirecting or subverting the authority of the image which has already been posited:

> In a house where no one knows each other's name,
> A zone where gardens overgrow and privet rankles –
> It stinks in summer and it blinds the panes.

There is a similar use in 'Ballywaire', with the lines "Through gunfire, night arrests and searches – / The crossroads loony smashed to bits –"; again these dashes allow the voice in the poem to become more severe or subjective, and thus they are already performing a function of allowing Paulin to switch the tone of a poem; though still acting to double-down on rather than open up the lyric line.

In Paulin's second collection, *The Strange Museum* (1980), the dash continues to serve the purpose of allowing for a change in register. In 'In the Lost Province', Paulin moves from an external narrative to an internal one through deployment of the dash: "As it comes back, brick by smoky brick, / I say to myself – strange I lived there". By the 1983 collection *Liberty Tree*, this same use of the dash is still in place and yet Paulin also seems to be using it as a way of altering a poem's point of view as well. So in 'Desertmartin', we're in the head of the 'I' of the poem for the line "I drive across it with a powerless knowledge –" and then the focus seems to shift, almost to a wide-angled shot, when we get to "The owl of Minerva in a hired car". In 'Manichean Geography II', the reader is told of "The slack wind – warm, trammelled –": here, again, there is a shift in focus – from external observation of the wind to feeling like one is inside it – yet the dash still works to reinforce rather than develop the image.

By the time one arrives at *Fivemiletown* (1987), Paulin's use of the dash, and what it is allowing the poems to do, is starting to expand. In 'The Bungalow on the Unapproved Road', the dash allows the poem to switch from third-person observation to first-person opinion ("The headboard was padded / with black vinyl – / just the ugliest thing / I'd seen in a long time"); though there is still that expected surety, particularly in comparison to a similar poem in *Love's Bonfire*, 'A Day with Two Anniversaries', in which the authority of the voice is constantly shifting and questioning itself.

In another *Fivemiletown* poem, 'Peacetime', we encounter the word "no" after a dash: "of the heavy trousers – / no wallet"; this feels like an important usage as it lays the groundwork for future instances in which the dash subverts or questions the lyric line, though in this case it is still serving the traditional purpose of adding a coda to the description. In 'Matins' from *Walking a Line* (1994), the gradual shift continues, with the phrase "you could hardly call them fields" following a dash; this is a softer version of the technique which appears in *Love's Bonfire* when, in 'A Spruce New Colour', Paulin writes:

> to the young man
> – a Presbyterian –
> who – I don't want to say *hangs* –
> who walks in the song

In this poem, alongside a deepening of description, the dash also enables Paulin to give an aside to the reader, framed as a negative ("I don't want to say..."). This allows the idea to be planted in the reader's mind without it having to be directly said within the poem itself. A similar technique is deployed in 'Air Plane', also from *Walking a Line*, in which Paulin writes "in its box of / – I should say sky – / in its box of air". The technique has not yet reached the point of outright contradiction, but it is here allowing Paulin to pose an alternative while still then carrying on with the original intention of the line. The dash, as has been consistent throughout the body of Paulin's work, is used as a 'but' rather than a way of layering: a slight diversion, a suggestion of something else creeping in.

It is through the voice of Churchill in the poem that bears his name, from *The Invasion Handbook* (2002), that we see the dash emerging as something which can facilitate the pulling-back from authorial impregnability of tone:

> I found Halifax had preceded me
> like a secondguesser
> or an ample
> familiar ghost
> robed in ermine
> – or was it Chamberlain's ghost
> his ghost to be

Here the dash becomes a hinge on which the second-guessing, unsure tone can swing in and out of the voice of any given poem.

If a dash were appropriate to begin a sentence in an essay, I'd deploy one here because I want to change tack – and ask, what's the point? Why get so exercised about a dash? First of all, there's no one who uses it like Paulin does, so subtly but with such resounding effects. Secondly, that shift from an image being compounded and confirmed, dug deeper into but ultimately validated, towards images that never seem sure, which always shift, is something that I believe is vital for poets to learn from and take into their own poetry.

In a 2002 article in *Literature and Theology*, discussing, among other things, Paulin's relationship to Hazlitt, Patricia Horton comments that:

> in attempting to step outside the subjectivism, irrationality and excess which the imagination represents, Paulin leaves himself trapped in a materialistic world which excludes any possibility of the mystical, the spiritual, the transcendent. His work can be read as an on-going struggle to resolve such tensions, a striving towards that seemingly paradoxical entity, the republican imagination.

Earlier she speaks of Paulin's "anxieties about the aesthetic". Horton's concerns are specifically religious and political, yet they can also help to shed light on the craft of Paulin's work. What others have called an "ambivalence", Horton would characterise as a "struggle", yet both words suggest an oscillation between differing perspectives, in Horton's view in service of moving towards this "paradoxical entity, the republican imagination"; perhaps the poems in *Love's Bonfire* have grown more comfortable sitting in this imaginative paradox.

Horton's later notion that "Paulin's representations undermine the notion that history has any one direction or singular narrative structure" are important to consider. So too her assertion that, in an interview with Eamonn Hughes, Paulin is "charting his own move away from empiricism with its emphasis on experience, observation and practice". Horton sees this enacted in *Fivemiletown*, but seemingly more in terms of what the poems are saying rather than how they are saying them. The "relativistic tone" she finds Hughes ascribing to *Fivemiletown* is still played out structurally with dashes which compound and add depth to images or thoughts, rather than contradicting them. The subjects might have shifted to a place of greater ambivalence, or struggle (depending on which critic you ask), but the poems, for all their candour of tone and startling clarity, are still clinging to their empiricism in terms of craft. It isn't until *Love's*

Bonfire, after fleeting test-runs in earlier poems, that Paulin feels able to call into question not the surety of history or the empiricism of truth, but the authorial voice in the poem.

Elmer Kennedy-Andrews gives us a brilliant turn of phrase when discussing Paulin's work in her book *Writing Home: Poetry and Place in Northern Ireland, 1968–2008*, commenting that:

> His own poetic practice, full of glitches and skelfs, is such a writing against the grain. Constantly, he is engaged in a deliberate effort to estrange and disrupt, to turn the poem into a vehicle of defamiliarisation, scandal and permanent critique.

'Skelf', a great colloquial synonym for 'splinter', gives us a wonderful way of thinking about what this article has thus far been calling the dash – indeed the marks Paulin makes by way of interjection or to transform his poems have the visual quality of a small splinter, lodged into the lyric line. Since Kennedy-Andrews' commentary on Paulin, it would seem that Paulin has turned this "effort to estrange and disrupt" onto the poet himself, attempting to estrange, disrupt and defamiliarise the authority of the poet-voice who is speaking.

. . .

The opening poem of *Love's Bonfire*, 'A Day with Two Anniversaries', starts the collection as it means to go on: "Our aim – no mine –". Whereas earlier Paulin might have used the dash to look deeper into the "aim", this poem offers one declarative up to the reader and then immediately undercuts it, calling into question the veracity of the coming narrative, indeed of the rest of the poems to come in the book; it reins in the poet's initial impulse to speak for more than just himself: the voice quickly recedes, coming back to just speaking for the self, rather than any grander purpose. So too a few lines later when, after the speaker has hit a badger, we are given "(couldn't – didn't – stop)"; here we get the dash but also the parenthesis, a doubling of the undercutting of the line which once more calls into question the narrative: is it that the speaker *couldn't* stop in time, or simply that he *didn't*?

The third poem in the collection, and one we have already encountered, 'A Spruce New Colour', begins with a line that seems to speak to that idea: "It all depends on your point of view / but from mine –". Straight away

Paulin is giving up the authoritative voice of the poet that might seek to speak for all people, or certain socio-geographical groupings of people, and places the coming statements squarely in the realms of his own personal opinion. Even this personal opinion is not, however, to be trusted:

> [...] – and I know that men
> can mistake colours and shades
> – from mine the new suspen-
> sion bridge at Toome is puce
> – puce or maybe lavender –

The bridge is a definite article, but its colour cannot be categorically stated, nor its shape, which could be "curved" or "semi-circular"; later a previous bridge is even reconsidered as "the bridge that stood in for the older one". Again the dash sparks these changes of direction. The only definite thing that Paulin doesn't question his own view of is the "police station / built like a barracks behind high walls and screens"; the physical remnants of a violent history are definite; but any other attempts to describe the landscape and its architecture can only be personal conjecture; history has its definite undeniable buildings, and actions, but the truth of them is malleable, and claimable by either side.

'A Spruce New Colour' is perhaps the poem busiest with these self-corrections, but there are others in the collection as well. In 'Kissing Ms Khosa', Paulin corrects himself: "Tip is touch / – as in tiptoe / or – better – on tiptoe"; again, where the dash might previously have been used to compound or solidify an image, it is here suggesting that language itself is a malleable, perhaps even contested space. 'The Thin Hem' presents more of a traditional use of the dash for Paulin – like those in his most recent books before *Love's Bonfire* – with its opening remark, "Maybe she's intending to pray", undercut and countered with "– no I can't – can't pray – it's such a drag". Here the dash is used as a hinge to swing another voice into the poem, adding depth to the perspective rather than contradicting it entirely. In 'Donegal Naif' it seems as though Paulin is already so settled into his use of the dash as a contradictory force that he begins to have fun with it, almost mocking his own, more serious uses of it earlier in the collection:

Some hairs off a donkey
– or some hairs off of a donkey
– its tail not its hide

This is a self-correction that seems to pre-empt the words of a critic or pedantic reader, and is a lighter use of the technique than one sees elsewhere in the collection.

In *The Secret Life of Poems*, published in 2008, a year before *Love's Bonfire*, Paulin opens:

Poetry begins in speech [...] it moves from there into the imagination and life of common people – into rhymes, riddles, traditional songs – and is then sometimes collected so that it moves from oral tradition, communal memory, into print.

The shift from speech and oral tradition, where many versions of the same thing exist, into communal memory which, by its very nature, will never be uniform, and then into print, fits with the notion that there can never really be one poetic definite which any given poem must follow on its way to the 'poetic truth'; people will have spoken of an event, a place, a time differently, they will each have differing memories of a particular moment.

Love's Bonfire sees Paulin move beyond the dash as a way of layering or deepening an image, and into a space where it can undercut the authority of any given lyric line; such is the confidence with which Paulin is deploying this new approach, that he is beginning to subvert it, to satirise it within the later poems in the collection. It is a technique that allows for the abandonment of authorial certainty and moves away from the poet as a teller of only one truth, which paradoxically moves a poem closer to the 'poetic truth' that Higgins mentions, because it feels much more honest. In a country that is facing renewed questions over its future in the wake of the referendum, it is a technique that offers great scope for the representation of "communal memory", however fallible and unsure that may well be.

Tom Paulin, New Selected Poems, *Faber, £12.99, ISBN 9780571307999*
Tom Paulin, Love's Bonfire, *Faber, £12.99, ISBN 9780571271535*

Prose from Poetry

WILLING TO BE RECKLESS

On Marianne Moore's New Collected Poems

Ange Mlinko

It was Robert Frost who said, in a letter, "in verse as in trapeze performance is all". Is it any surprise then to read of Marianne Moore that she kept a trapeze in her house – "mystifying visitors", writes her biographer, Linda Leavell? Moore was a consummate performer in her work (the biography is even called *Holding on Upside Down*), and she admired athletes in particular, having famously pitched the first ball of the season at Yankee Stadium in 1968, and having written the liner notes for *I Am the Greatest!* by Cassius Clay (aka Muhammad Ali). Among the best pieces of prose she wrote was an essay on Anna Pavlova, not because she was a balletomane, but because something about the dancer's "persuasion of contrasts" spoke to her own sense of artistry: "undogmatic decisiveness, strength of foot with lightness of body; technical proficiency with poetic feeling; aloofness and simplicity in one who had chosen as her art that most exposed form of self-expression, dancing." These traits abound in Moore's poetry; I turn a page at random for a sample and land on 'The Mind is an Enchanting Thing':

is an enchanted thing
    like the glaze on a
katydid-wing
        subdivided by sun
        till the nettings are legion.
Like Gieseking playing Scarlatti;

like the apteryx-awl
    as a beak, or the
kiwi's rain-shawl
        of haired feathers, the mind
        feeling its way as though blind,
walks along with its eyes on the ground.

Poetry's great modernists were all performers jostling for supremacy on the "make it new" stage, but they were in rare agreement about Moore (including that performer of austerity, Frost, striding the modernist faultline). Ezra Pound, as ever performing the impresario, championed her as early as 1915. W.H. Auden, who performed the schoolmaster, wrote of her: "there are very few poets who give me more pleasure to read." Wallace Stevens, who performed the dandy, reviewed her work in terms that could have applied to his own: "Miss Moore's reality is significant. An aesthetic integration is a reality." H.D., who performed the Delphic oracle, wrote that Moore's poems were "frail, yet as all beautiful things are, absolutely hard". With the help of T.S. Eliot and her heiress lover Bryher, H.D. surprised Moore with the secret publication of her first collection in 1921; Eliot brought out a later selection in 1935, and wrote the preface for it. William Carlos Williams wrote to her: "Why should I not speak in superlatives [...] there is no work in verse being done in any language which I can read which I find more to my liking and which I believe to be so thoroughly excellent." He, along with Pound and H.D., had missed meeting the self-styled "Byronesque" redhead in college, from 1906 to 1909, while the women attended Bryn Mawr and the men swanned around UPenn.

This unanimity among her most illustrious peers in the heyday of modernism is one justification for recent corrective scholarship on Moore. In 2013, Linda Leavell published a revelatory new biography. In 2016, Farrar, Straus and Giroux reissued her groundbreaking book *Observations* with an introduction by Leavell, which restored the original versions of poems that Moore had suppressed over the course of a career-long revision process. And now we have a *New Collected Poems*, edited by Heather Cass White, which also prioritises poems in the forms originally encountered in their books, and replaces both Moore's own *Complete Poems* from 1967 and the 2005 *The Poems of Marianne Moore*, overseen by Grace Schulman, which, among other things, obscured *Observations* and front-loaded Moore's juvenilia.

What was Moore's verbal trapeze-work like, then? She was a genius metaphor-maker to begin with, but it was her daring use of form that drew gasps. Her only free verse was written between 1921 and 1924, producing masterpieces like 'Marriage' and 'An Octopus'; more commonly she worked in *sui generis* stanzas that draped highly wrought sentences (think Henry James, an early influence) onto a syllabic armature, replete with innovative end rhymes (often sight rhymes), that retained the look of poetry (slightly more angular, "stiffly geometrical", said Harriet Monroe rather disapprovingly) while sounding nothing like metrical English verse. At the same time, she was an early adopter of the collage method – the signal modernist invention – interpolating her authorial voice with quotes whose provenance weren't always clear, even after notes were added to the back of the book. Sometimes they were quotes from the diaries and letters of great writers; sometimes they were taken from anonymous news stories and pamphlets; sometimes they were lifted from ordinary conversation – her mother talking, say. This self-interruption, this choral effect, is most associated with Eliot and Pound, but no one made it sound as witty and conversational as Moore. (Auden: "Uncomprehending as I was, I felt attracted by the tone of voice.") She could be funny, self-deprecating (picturing herself as an "intramural rat" for instance) and tart, titling a poem 'To Be Liked by You Would Be a Calamity'. Moore said, of her years as a reviewer then editor at the avant-garde magazine *The Dial*, "I think that individuality was the great thing. We were not conforming to anything. We certainly didn't have a policy, except I remember hearing the word 'intensity' very often. A thing must have intensity." She elaborated:

Wallace Stevens was really very much annoyed at being cataloged, categorized, and compelled to be scientific about what he was doing – to give satisfaction, to answer the teachers. He wouldn't do that. I think the same of William Carlos Williams. I think he wouldn't make so much of the great American language if he were plausible and tractable. That's the beauty of it – he is willing to be reckless. If you can't be that, what's the point of the whole thing?

Intensity, but an attractive tone. Hardness – in the sense of both difficulty and unsentimentality – but recklessness. This is what moved her peers, and what drew criticism from more conventional readers (who accused her of obscurity and lack of emotion – of course! – but also of formal incompetence). As you read her poetry chronologically, from the experimental *Observations* through the later work, you sense that you are watching Moore figure out what she was about – her categories, if you will – and once she did, the recklessness ebbed away. She also grew more accommodating – "tractable" – writing for occasions and commissions, with lucidity but with less bite. If we think of, say, Emily Dickinson as our lyric poet, on the order of Sappho with her lone-voiced, private intensities, we might think of Moore in her later years as our Pindar: public, choral, odic. She did, after all, write a victory ode for the Brooklyn Dodgers, and America knew her as an icon in a tricorne hat and cape – on television even, as a guest on the *Today* show, a guest on the *Tonight* show, paired with Mickey Spillane in a commercial for Braniff Airways. This is not an unusual career trajectory (for all kinds of artists), but the constant rewriting of one's work doesn't just create a quandary for editors, it distorts the past. And the past, like poetry, is usually more complicated and surprising than we like to believe.

. . .

Marianne Moore was born in 1887 in a suburb of St Louis. One of the piquant coincidences of modern poetry is that T.S. Eliot was born in the vicinity less than a year later; had their grandfathers not been ministers of rival sects – hers Presbyterian, his Unitarian – they might have met in childhood. As it was, her grandfather died when Moore was eight, and her mother, Mary Warner Moore, moved her and her brother to Carlisle, in south central Pennsylvania, where she lived until matriculating at Bryn Mawr.

Moore never mentioned her father; her fellow poets wondered about that, and about the unusual closeness between her and her mother and brother. Leavell's biography clears up the mystery of paternity. Marianne and (John) Warner Moore never knew their father; John Milton Moore had had a psychotic breakdown within a couple of years of his impulsive marriage to Mary Warner, and died in an institution when Marianne was sixteen. The facts of his case are brutal: plagued with religious mania to the end of his days, he amputated his own right hand in accordance with the scripture in Matthew 5:30 – "And if thy right hand offend thee, cut it off."

Mary Warner had lost her mother in infancy, to the typhoid epidemic that swept Gettysburg in the aftermath of the ghastly civil war battle. Orphanhood and single-motherhood were mitigated by a small family trust, extended kin, and the stable milieu of genteel, educated progressivism both in Kirkwood and Carlisle. Mary ended up a teacher at the girls' school that Marianne attended, and found herself romanced by a younger woman, Mary Norcross, an educator and Bryn Mawr alumna. The two were lovers for a decade while Marianne and Warner were growing up. The family read books like *The Wind in the Willows* to one another, adopting nicknames for each other from its characters; daily prayer and Sunday service were also features of the household. While this Christian lesbian ménage confounds our present categories, it may explain why Moore sought the safety of her immediate family all her life, while maintaining a public stance of profound nonconformism.

Moore started writing poetry at Bryn Mawr, where she was not a stellar student – biology, not English, was her best subject. Still, she was popular, and her teachers attended to her diligently. After graduation she became the kind of alert young woman who, though isolated from her poetic peers, would make her way to Alfred Stieglitz's 291 gallery to see experimental painting and photography, and send her poetic efforts to experimental little magazines like *The Egoist*, *Others*, and, yes, Harriet Monroe's *Poetry*. H.D. saw those first poems in *The Egoist* in 1915 and recognised her fellow alumna's name. They struck up a correspondence and a friendship; by 1921, impatient with Moore's reluctance to publish a book, she conspired to have a small one printed in London without her knowledge. Moore was unhappy with the unauthorised *Poems*, and it was poorly reviewed. She had another chance at a 'first' book in 1924 with *Observations*, an expanded version of *Poems* which now contained masterpieces like 'Marriage' and 'An Octopus'.

Observations was reprinted with slight changes in 1925; the one ominous note was a shortened version of the famous poem 'Poetry', which continued to contract and expand over the years, pythonlike. I can barely quote its first line, "I, too, dislike it" – a line put to as many false uses as Auden's "poetry makes nothing happen". If Moore found it difficult to sum up her *ars poetica* in one definitive poem, she needn't have worried so much. *Observations* as a whole constitutes a prismatic exploration of art: what it is, what it means to create it, and what *déformations professionelles* it visits on its creators. Animal and plant specimens are presented as creatures and creators both, having to adapt to conditions they have inherited, not made. These solutions are then praised as beautiful: the chameleon "snap[s] the spectrum up for food"; the snail has a "principle that is hid"; the rat's wit is "too brisk to be inspected". There's a now-you-see-me-now-you-don't aspect to all the animal-artist's qualities, since both display and camouflage are essential to survival in the wild.

Actually I shouldn't reduce Moore's approbations to mere praise, "beautiful"; more often she'll declare her object a "curio", cognate with curious, connoting something both odd and worthy of attention. "Curiouser and curiouser!" said Alice in Wonderland; Auden, who playfully divided writers into "Alices" and "Mabels", identified Moore as an Alice (along with Austen, Montaigne, Marvell, and Woolf). In 'The Monkey Puzzler', Moore identifies with the "true curio", the Chilean monkey puzzle tree (she changes "puzzle" into "puzzler", object into agent). It is an ancient, spiky thing – a living fossil, in fact, and Moore wonders: "One is at a loss, however, to know why it should be here, / in this morose part of the earth – / to account for its origin at all; / but we prove, we do not explain our birth." Likewise in 'Roses Only', Moore instructs the artist: "You do not seem to realise that beauty is a liability rather than / an asset [...] / your thorns are the best part of you." "Are they weapons or scalpels?" she asks another totem in 'Those Various Scalpels'. It is this "hardness" that H.D. recognised and praised, the presence of the claw or tooth, blade or spine in the language. In her essay 'Feeling and Precision', Moore acknowledges this: "The lion's leap would be mitigated almost to harmlessness if the lion were clawless, so precision is both impact and exactitude, as with surgery."

Much of the great pleasure of a Moore poem, circa 1925, was in the way it played with argument. If the arguments had much to do with the identity between the creator and the created – *How does a thing exist – a snail, a vase, me?* – a sort of aesthetic ontology – it was really in the mimicry of debate that she made her points. The argument is usually *between* sentences rather than advanced by the sentences. Or the argument is begun rhetorically, then carried dialectically by opposing images (a "persuasion of contrasts", as she said of Pavlova). This can be frustrating if you're looking for the manifesto outright. Take 'Marriage': Moore's background, and her rejection of marriage – specifically, a proposal by Scofield Thayer, her editor at *The Dial* – ought to have yielded a poem giving critics of the institution powerful ammunition, but it's not that, despite some choice quotes ("experience attests / that men have power / and sometimes one is made to feel it" – yes, but "a wife is a coffin"). Moore's note for her poem 'Picking and Choosing' steers us to Eliot's essay on Henry James; it's the one where he accuses James of having "a mind so fine that no idea could violate it". Perhaps Moore was giving us the key right here – she would not violate her poems with mere ideas, though she would pantomime them, dance with them (Pound: "the dance of the intellect among words"), and then abandon them at the altar.

Yet tendencies and innuendoes tell us a lot about predilections. One of the unfortunate results of Moore's later obscuration of *Observations* is that its covert gender critique could not be gauged by feminist poets like Adrienne Rich, who would not see past her "maidenly, elegant, intellectual, discreet" persona. 'Marriage' may be intellectual and discreet – maidenly and elegant I'm not so sure:

> that striking grasp of opposites
> opposed each to the other, not to unity,
> which in cycloid inclusiveness
> has dwarfed the demonstration
> of Columbus with the egg –
> a triumph of simplicity –
> that charitive Euroclydon
> of frightening disinterestedness
> which the world hates

The Euroclydon is a destructive Mediterranean wind that may have shipwrecked St Paul – he of 1 Corinthians 7:9: "But if they cannot contain, let them marry: for it is better to marry than to burn" – on his way to Rome. The form of the Euroclydon is cyclonic; it is the wedding ring. The poem too is cyclonic; not only does it circle around its subject, it presents "circular traditions" as a theme and offers chiasmi and tautologies in a long free-verse excursus that exceeds the bounds of "elegant" poetry as defined by almost anyone in 1924.

There are two peculiar poems about fathers that defy authority beneath their deft surfaces. 'Silence' comes right after 'Marriage' in the book (an ironic comment right there, no?). The first line goes "My father used to say..." but Marianne didn't know her father; her endnotes tell us that she is quoting a friend, a professor of hygiene at Wellesley, A.M. Homans. And then, by an act of collage, she quotes Edmund Burke and makes an ironic epigram applicable to parents and children: "Nor was he insincere in saying, 'Make my house your inn.' / Inns are not residences." Thus the Enlightenment thinker is collapsed with the hygiene professor's father, collapsed with the speaker's father, the speaker supposedly being Moore, who had no father. The layers of fictiveness are mind-boggling for so short a poem, and just as ironic – and funnier – is the other father poem, '"He Wrote the History Book"'. It takes as its donné a child's solecism, "My father wrote the history book." (As if there were one!) "Authentically / brief," Moore almost drawls to the child, "Thank you for showing me / your father's autograph." As a further riposte, she rhymes it with *chaff*.

Maybe it sounds tendentious to say there's gender critique in the book – there's an anti-authoritarian streak, and it comes out in these poems as well as in 'To a Steam Roller', 'To Military Progress', 'Pedantic Literalist', and 'Critics and Connoisseurs'. As befits a book largely about aesthetics, a great many of the poems deal with judging. We may deduce that she is addressing men in power, but she lets the images and their connotations imply rather than accuse. When feminists dismissed her as a "maidenly", unthreatening token in the male-dominated world of avant-gardists, they could not have known that she was raised by lesbians and took on the male pronoun in the family's private language (the over thirty thousand archived letters between Mary, Marianne, and Warner attest to this); they could not have read 'An Intra-mural Rat', the first poem in the book, as a self-portrait: "You make me think of many men / Once met to be forgot again." Here was gender fluidity on the page *avant la lettre* – or perhaps Tiresias, if, per another poem, 'The Past is the Present'.

In the end, the enigmatic and energetic poems in *Observations* evade the intelligence "almost successfully", as Stevens's adage would have it. The comparison is acute. Both poets counter the violence of reality with the violence of the imagination; Stevens fashioned this notion in the thirties, but he could well have gotten it from 'Sea Unicorns and Land Unicorns', the final poem in *Observations* and a brilliant study in symbolic counterpoint (the poem takes as its premise the notion, lifted from a sixteenth-century privateer's explorations of Florida, that if a land is found to harbour lions then it follows that unicorns must inhabit it too, since lions and unicorns are nemeses in legend). *Harmonium* was published only the previous year, in 1923. *Observations* doesn't have the same name recognition, the same reputation as a 'best first book' of the twentieth century, but both the Farrar, Straus and Giroux reissue and the *New Collected Poems* should help to change that. It is every bit as strange, every bit as preoccupied as Stevens's *chef d'oeuvre* with its own becoming, its own reason for being, its own aesthetic repleteness. It also celebrates the fun and joy in making that animates *Harmonium*. Consider too that he was forty-three, she thirty-seven when these first books were published. They are secret siblings, chaste yet resplendent.

· · ·

After *Observations*, Moore went silent for a few years. She had taken on editorial responsibilities at the little magazine *The Dial*, where she had been a regular reviewer, and had a spell of ill health. Both she and her mother would take to bed frequently in the next few decades, with ailments ranging from bursitis to bronchitis. Moore had always been delicate in fact – the aforementioned trapeze had been prescribed for her scoliosis, and she was chronically underweight (there is even speculation about anorexia). But then Moore began a few more masterpieces that would appear in her next book, *Selected Poems*, edited by Eliot: 'The Steeple-Jack', 'The Jerboa' and 'The Plumet Basilisk', to name just three. These poems expand and amplify the discoveries Moore made in *Observations*. They have that rarefied strangeness of her best poems: the "eight stranded whales" of the town in 'The Steeple-Jack', the "pine-cone / or fircone – with holes for a fountain" that launches 'The Jerboa'. The *objets d'art* seem productively otiose (like 'No Swan So Fine'), the animals unpretty but resourceful. 'The Plumet Basilisk' contains some of her most agile writing, surprising in its line breaks, its pacing:

> Among tightened wires,
> minute noises swell
> and change as in the woods' acoustic shell
>
> they will, with trees as
> avenues of steel

to veil invisibleness ears must feel –
black opal emerald opal
emerald – the prompt-delayed loud-
low chromatic listened-for down-
scale which Swinburne called in prose, the
noiseless music that hangs about
the serpent when it stirs or springs.

I hear not Swinburne so much as Hopkins's sprung rhythm. Moore admired Hopkins, citing his exemplary line, "about some lambs he had seen frolicking in a field, 'It was as though it was the ground that tossed them.'" It hearkens to her image of poetry as a "lion's leap"– perhaps she had a mind to revise Hopkins for a more Darwinian century.

Selected Poems, like *Observations*, was received with ovations by her peers, but Moore still found it difficult to place her work with major magazines like the *New Yorker*, which had by the forties embraced her protégée, Elizabeth Bishop. "Technical virtuosity is not the essential nourishment we need at this time," Moore wrote philosophically, on the cusp of WWII. Her remark reminds me that she titled one of her essays 'Humility, Concentration, and Gusto' – a triumvirate of virtues that could go down with Bishop's "accuracy, spontaneity, mystery" and Stevens's "It must be abstract", "it must change", "it must give pleasure". But humility can be taken too far, and Moore's poems in the forties began a slow creep toward détente with the reading public.

And her mother. For it remains the overwhelming fact of Marianne Moore's life that when her mother's lover left her for another woman, in 1910, Marianne was called home to comfort her, and remained under her roof – first in Carlisle, then Greenwich Village, then Brooklyn – for the next thirty-seven years, until the supposedly frail older woman died at the age of eighty-five. And not only under her roof, but in a shared bed. They rarely spent a night apart; after her spirited college years ("Byronesque", although schoolgirl crushes, one on William James's daughter, were about the extent of it), there is not even the hint of a love interest for the rest of her life. "Love is more important than being in love, as memories of childhood testify," Moore remarked.

Even more appallingly, this domestic arrangement all but ensured that Mary Warner Moore was Marianne's first reader for all those decades. Leavell sees Moore's work as enacting, right from the start, the struggle for freedom that eluded her in her mother's grasp, and at first she didn't mind much that the poems eluded her mother's grasp in her stead. Not only did Mary dislike Marianne's 'An Octopus' – which John Ashbery, for one, regarded as her greatest poem – but declared her daughter's first book "a veiled Mohammedan woman". When world events began their excruciating pressure in the late thirties, the women would read the newspaper to each other. Mary's Presbyterian-schoolmistressy piety surely must have collaborated with Axis forces to wear down her daughter's defenses: 'What Are Years' (1941) starts off with the question, "What is our innocence, / what is our guilt?" And though it spoke to the nation, as it were, and was subsequently anthologised, it is squarely within the bounds of 'fine writing', lacking an imaginative dimension. With every passing decade, Moore's poems contained less and less of the thorny and the furtive. To gauge the difference, take 'O to Be a Dragon', from her 1959 book of the same name. It hearkens back to Moore's 'To a Chameleon' (1916):

> Hid by the august foliage and fruit of the grape vine,
> Twine,
>> Your anatomy
>>> Round the pruned and polished stem,
>>>> Chameleon.
>>>> Fire laid upon
>>> An emerald as long as
>> The Dark King's massy
> One,
> Could not snap the spectrum up for food as you have done.

Here are the hallmarks of modernism with its odd juxtapositions. The poem is in couplets but not in isometric lines. It mixes perfect and imperfect rhymes. Its non-accentual-syllabic metre doesn't sound musical (until the last line offers itself as a swift, sure hexameter with a caesura in the middle). One might say that it's in double couplets, since it is composed of two sentences, and the two sentences finally rhyme (chameleon/have done). That the middle couplet carries the rhyme but divides the sentences suggests the twining (or twinning) of the reptile with its branch. The final, negative image of the emerald that *can't* "snap the spectrum up for food" flashes a fugitive defiance at "the Dark King".

But what we get in 1959 is watered-down children's-book verse:

If I, like Solomon, [...]
could have my wish –
   my wish [...] O to be a dragon,
a symbol of the power of Heaven – of silkworm
size or immense; at times invisible.
      Felicitous phenomenon!

"Felicitous phenomenon!" – ? Trade secret: a pinch of alliteration will distract from the blandness of the dish. Yet 'O to Be a Dragon' is trademark anthology-friendly Moore, appearing in *Life* magazine in 1967 under the gushing heading, "Four poems that show her mind's wide range". In all those years, there wasn't a poem to rival 'Marriage', or that broke from the formula of animal- and object-lesson.

In her later years, Moore attracted not only more readers, but invitations to read and lecture, magazine profiles (*Life*, the *New Yorker*, *Sports Illustrated*), television appearances, rich patronesses, and of course prizes. She returned the favour with poems that celebrated pop culture (Yul Brynner, the Brooklyn Dodgers), and answered to commissions or occasions. Wasn't Auden doing much the same thing at the time – writing poems on cuisine? But no one wrote an essay about Moore on the order of Philip Larkin's 'What's Become of Wystan?'. When she died in her sleep at age eighty-four, the headline appeared above the fold on the *New York Times*, and President Nixon issued a statement about the death of "one of our most distinguished poets".

Moore's final legacy to her readers was her 1967 *Complete Poems*. "Mendaciously titled," says Cass White, "that collection is anything but complete, containing only just over half of the poems she actually published during her life. Perhaps more importantly, many of the poems it does contain are extensively altered versions of poems she first wrote decades earlier." Leavell adds, "The *Complete Poems* presents her final intentions but not necessarily her most compelling ones." Both Cass White and Leavell, in restoring original versions of *Observations*, follow on the heels of Robin G. Schulze's *Becoming Marianne Moore: The Early Poems, 1907–1924* (2002), in which she presents a facsimile version of the 1924 *Observations*, as well as facsimiles of poems published in college and little magazines. Schulze's introduction gives a condensed version of Moore's publication history, and shows how Moore – and modernist – scholarship was warped by reliance on the older Moore's truncated selection of her oeuvre.

To ask why Moore was such a destructive reviser seems somehow both futile and obvious. Poets revise because we can – we are the petty tyrants of our work – and because we are attracted to a form that in its compactness offers the illusion of perfectibility. It is also, quite simply, much easier to revise than to create something out of nothing; revising gives one the illusion of productivity in the face of the fickle muse. Auden too was compulsive about his revisions; his literary executor, Edward Mendelson, has restored two important poems to Auden's canon which the poet tried to suppress ('Spain' and the renowned 'September 1, 1939'). Mendelson refers to the "gothic-tower model" of revision:

> Here the original conception is merely a rough sketch [...] The work is never entirely finished, because the author continually finds weak links that need repairs or improvements, and the work continues to be altered – even after the author's death – by editors and publishers, sometimes to the point where a later century calls in professional restorers to undo the mistaken restorations and doubtful improvements made by earlier centuries.

Grace Schulman, who knew Moore, thought that she had "a predilection for change", evident in her poems' subject matter. Yet Moore also allegedly told her, "I aspire to have a taproot, but I don't have one." What she meant by that is up for debate: did her treatment of her poetry as a medium in flux have to do with her semi-orphaned childhood? Over-reliance on her mother? Or was poetry's innate "negative capability" a source of anxiety rather than, as it was for Keats, a source of "Beauty [that] overcomes every other consideration"? It might be that, as with Auden (and contra Arcadian Keats), Moore's Protestantism made moral, rational demands on her poetry that poetry, in all its generative anarchy, cannot sustain. The revisions were an attempt to reconcile them.

It was only in the last couple of decades that the principles of "final authorial intention", which guided mid-century editors of the Anglo-American school (related to New Criticism), made room for theories of "textual instability", which has given us, among other things, the variorum edition of Emily Dickinson's poems. Dickinson scholars have been undoing layers of editorial intervention, revealing an even more experimental, perhaps indeterminate, poet than we'd dreamed. Moore's case – the undoing of authorial intervention – reverses the scenario. Someday there will be a variorum edition of Marianne Moore. Yet the fact remains that most of us don't need or want to read twenty versions of a poem: we want the gasp of immediate recognition, "a few 'strong wrinkles' puckering the / skin between the ears", as Moore put it in – irony of ironies – 'Picking and Choosing'. Someone must do the picking and choosing, requiring exquisite sensitivity: nerves over intellection, pleasure in puzzlement, an appreciation for the "lion's leap". "My aim is simple," writes Cass White, "I have here presented Moore's poems as they were when she first wrote and published them, not as she later revised them." It must be odd, though – perhaps unprecedented – to be put in the position of having to rescue poems from their *makar*, a fabulous creature, which has been known to cannibalise itself.

Marianne Moore, New Collected Poems, *ed. Heather Cass White, Farrar, Straus and Giroux, $30, ISBN 9780374221041. Available in the UK published by Faber, ISBN 9780571315338.*

CLOSER

Douglas Dunn, The Noise of a Fly, *Faber, £14.99,*
ISBN 9780571333813
Penelope Shuttle, Will You Walk A Little Faster, *Bloodaxe, £9.95,*
ISBN 9781780373539

Kayo Chingonyi on perspective and reflection

. . .

In *The Noise of a Fly* Douglas Dunn's poetic speaker is often to be found, either implicitly or otherwise, addressing those younger than himself, whether he is offering advice in poems like 'A Teacher's Notes' or 'The Wash' or else speaking from a perspective informed by such things as the deaths of his contemporaries or shifts in social norms. It is no surprise that this speaker reflects more than once on a feeling of disorientation: "Closing a door on what was once my life, / My days, my work. Farewell, and so goodbye" ('Leaving the Office'); "Who lives there, in that land of the utter truth? / Is it one of the delusions of youth, // Or the delusions of age and adulthood? / Well, I don't know" ('The Nothing-But').

The interrogative mode of this latter passage is returned to in a number of the poems collected in this book, suggesting that age offers no final conclusions. The stanza break here illustrates this, undermining fixed notions of age and youth and instead arguing for the possibility that neither is the domain of "utter truth". If "utter" here means "complete or absolute" (OED) then the inference is that there is a confidence that comes with youth and one that comes with age and both might be misguided. So, while Dunn's poetic speaker is often didactic he might be so not out of confidence but out of insecurity, an insecurity that is reflected in the tone of the first passage quoted above. Though "what was once my life" seems hyperbolic it reflects on the feeling of loss attending retirement – when the wider culture offers few examples of what comes after. The metaphor used is particularly apt since a door conveys us across a threshold and we often close doors when taking our leave. This subtle resonance is a wonderful example of what Dunn is doing in the book as a whole: sounding a valedictory note while working out what comes next. Indeed 'working out' is another way of talking about what these poems do collectively; they reflect on a poet's reckoning with time.

While there is an important sense in which the poems looking back add context to the more exegetical aspects of the book, there are some moments where the modes of address, usually from an older speaker to a younger reader, become problematic. So it is with the poem 'Senex on Market Street', which argues for the right of an older, presumably male, spectator to comment on how young women look:

> There's something I must tell – need you know this? –
> I loved a woman who dressed as well as you;
> But I can't give the past false emphasis,
> For even old love is for ever new.
> > When she walked out she dulcified the air;
> > And so do you. To say so's only fair.

When this passage is read in the light of the first line of the poem, "Posh totty totter past on serious heels", the poem cannot do anything but objectify those it ostensibly seeks to praise. Consequently the poem offers not so much the epiphany it gestures towards with the use of the word "dulcified", as a reaffirmation of the notion that (straight, cis) maleness, and its stereotypical tropes, are the normative subjectivity. While this kind of myopia is not a frequent problem in the book, it does demonstrate an issue with the book's sense of its audience, a gap that might have been written further into. What if the poem's speaker had followed the impulse behind the question "need you know this?" and addressed men of his own generation and their sense[s] of entitlement instead?

"My life, I can't fool you, / you know me too well" begins the speaker in the opening poem of Penelope Shuttle's latest collection, a book that takes its title from the entreaty at the heart of contemporary life. And if the world around us seems always to be saying "hurry up", then this book exhorts its readers to slow down from time to time as well. So we have poems like 'My Life', quoted above, in which the speaker is in conversation with their own life which has become a person with a deep insight into the speaker's personality. Elsewhere this same focus on gaining perspective is reflected in a number of poems looking back, we assume, to childhood:

> My father
> of the sleety air
> my father of his silence
> his sword of stardust
> and ash
> as years go by   as if he'd never been
> ('My father promised me a sword')

The wonders of childhood are here in words such as "stardust" and in the speaker's viewpoint; the father is "of" the air, a magical being drawn from the elements. That these wonders give way eventually is the poem's main propositional content but this poem is a good example of how Shuttle's poems say things. The lineation favours a fluid, improvisational rhythm over a more fixed pattern and there is a lot of space in Shuttle's poems. This serves to fix an image in the mind and complicate and qualify that image as the poem unfolds. So, even though the end of the poem is expected and offers no new epiphany, the manner of getting there forces the reader to be present as they read, following clause after clause until the full picture is clear. In the process of reading the reader takes on the feeling of wonder that a child might have when trying to make sense of the adult world. This lends Shuttle's poems a liveliness that belies their focus on what is lost to time or the process of looking back into a life. Indeed the presentation of these poems in this way adds an idiosyncratic aspect to what in the hands of another poet might be a plainer, less nuanced, poem.

This fluid lineation is a hallmark of this book and contributes to an overall feeling that Shuttle is in perfect control of her material even when the speakers falter:

and I'm getting closer
and closer
to you
despite what people tell me
is the otherwise

('I often think')

but it can't be done
this looking back

('Streets and their childhoods')

Taken together these two passages are emblems of the book as a whole. On the one hand the impulse behind the poems is to address mortality, to face the passage of time and set the contemporary moment in context, and on the other hand there is a sense that looking back in order to do this might be a way of avoiding what is happening now. It is difficult not to align the speaker in 'I often think' with Shuttle, since we know of the loss to which she has returned often in her work, the death of her partner Peter Redgrove. Whether the speaker is or isn't the poet, what we know, outside of the poem, suggests that Shuttle has insight into what the poem contains. Given this information the poem becomes an exploration of the ways in which the dead stay with us, how we think of them and hold them in our bodies. This gives the words quoted in the passage above a dual resonance as both an expression of grief and perhaps of relief, also. There is an intimacy to a word like "closer" which for a moment takes us away from thoughts of mortality to dwell on what closeness means; the overlap of two different people forming a unity. While there is a hardness to the sentiment expressed in the latter passage quoted above, the book attempts what "can't be done" all the same and it is this that is one of its most emphatic statements: just because a thing cannot be done, that's not to say there's nothing interesting in the attempt.

Kayo Chingonyi is poetry editor at The White Review. *His first full-length collection is* Kumukanda *(Chatto, 2017).*

THE EMBASSY OF ANGELS

Danez Smith, Don't Call Us Dead, *Chatto, £10.99,*
ISBN 9781784742041
Cal Freeman, Fight Songs, *Eyewear, £10.99,*
ISBN 9781911335658
Ishion Hutchinson, House of Lords and Commons, *Faber, £12.99*
ISBN 9780571340149

Karen McCarthy Woolf on resilience, revolution and requiem

. . .

Tense, uncompromising and forcefully propelled by its subjects and their contexts, *Don't Call Us Dead* is a work of intimate and political urgency. Danez Smith writes of and for black America at a time when the systemic assault on black culture, lives and bodies is intensifying. Smith writes also as a gay man who is HIV positive. That the book's title is an imperative is apt, recalling Reni Eddo-Lodge's *Why I'm No Longer Talking to White People About Race* (2017) in its terse corrective. These poems articulate and resist the binary in favour of the Other and in so doing synthesise as protest lyric, requiem and charged vehicle of transformation. It's difficult to select a single quotation from the thematically iconic prose poem 'dear white america' to illustrate this point, as its identity (as epistle, as rant) and syntactical engine is fuelled by a breathless yet controlled, cumulative momentum. Given these ambitions, it emerges, at a single page, as a poem of some concision:

> i'm sick of calling your recklessness the law. each night, i count my
> brothers. & in the morning, when some do not survive to be counted,
> i count the holes they leave. i reach for black folks & touch only air.
> your master magic trick, America. now he's breathing, now he don't.
> abra-cadaver. white bread voodoo. sorcery you claim not to practice,
> hand my cousin a pistol to do your work.

The use of the ampersand and the lowercase lyric "i" is consistent
throughout, a convention that situates Smith within the embrace of queer
poetics as exemplified by bell hooks and Nikki Giovanni. At first glance
this might be interpreted solely as a means of establishing a literary lineage;
however, its linguistic effect resonates further when you hear Smith read:
the punctuation acting as performative score as much as it does a control
mechanism on the page.

Fierce though it may be, *Don't Call Us Dead* is textured in its registers.
In the delicate and tender opening sequence 'summer, somewhere', from
which the titular phrase is extracted, the speaker is a murdered youth,
who could be Emmett Till or Trayvon Martin, amongst many. He resides
in a place that is neither earth nor heaven, where "the forest is a flock of
boys / who never got to grow up // blooming into forever / afros like maple
crowns // reaching sap-slow toward sky".

Here and elsewhere, the embodied individual and collective self is set
against Nature as a metaphorical template that symbolises life, thwarted
yet enduring, as a means through which Smith conveys irony, hope and
despair. It is also a reminder that the black experience extends beyond the
urban. In this landscape the reader is invited to "imagine a tulip, upon
seeing a garden full of tulips, sheds its petals in disgust, prays some bee
will bring its pollen to a rose bush". ('& even the black guy's profile reads
sorry, no black guys'), or discover that "if snow fell, it'd fall black". It is a
place where blood flows through the book like a river, as a pathway
between life and death via God, where children "go out for sweets & come
back" ('summer, somewhere').

Cal Freeman's *Fight Songs* is also a work of witness, often, but not
exclusively focused around his native city, Detroit, as emblem of industrial
and urban decay, and by extension as synecdochic rendering of neo-capitalist
America at its apex/nadir. "Does it matter what I have seen?" the speaker

asks, in 'Epistle to an Athenian', a letter initially addressed to the Greek hero, Theseus:

> Each ephemeral city faces
> fire or deluge before becoming myth;
>
> they all disappear beneath
> the polished weight
> of their names—Atlantis, Carthage,
>
> Detroit—and the helmets clash.

Said helmets being those of the city's "bigot fathers" and "cops chomping / pseudo-legalese in black faces", who patrol a world where "An untold cocktail of chemicals // rides the east air" ('Fight Song to be Sung Between Trade Wars'). In this context, classical reference and literary allusion become germane to the project – a quality that comes as something of a relief, as the risk with environmentally alert work is an apocalyptic wallowing that overlooks or underestimates political affect.

It is in this spirit that Freeman evokes Blake in poems such as 'Epistle to the Innocent' and 'Epistle to a Scullery Boy'. In 'Fight Song of the Lazar House' the poet returns to his grandparents' former home, now inhabited by his uncle and a companion 'Cindy' who he finds "at the strip mall / methodically searching / the potted plants and / sidewalk cracks for butts", and whose kitchen is scattered with bottles of "Lithium, Haloperidol, / Zoloft, Oxycontin" – a list which substitutes the US opioid epidemic for Hogarth's 'Gin Lane'. This is an important poem because it positions its author as an insider, as opposed to voyeur or, heaven forbid, a tourist, as is the case in 'London', which, with its somewhat cursory surface, the collection would have been stronger without.

Freeman enlists an expansive vocabulary to relate matters of the anthropocene with varying degrees of success. There are moments when precision overwhelms the music, as in 'Genus Ephemera: Fight Song of the Fish Flies', a prose poem that ultimately capsizes under the weight of scientific data. Elsewhere, by contrast, the ecopoetic endeavour is deftly handled, as in 'Fight Song with Turtle and Mallard':

We can count the stoneflies
and catalogue frog croaks

and marvel at the elegiac numbers.

It gets tempting to call what's left
resilience [...]

Resilience, of the planet and its people, is a shared concern in Ishion Hutchinson's *House of Lords and Commons*, and one that emerges as a revolution that subverts from within. If Smith's sense of postcolonial urgency produces poems that proceed at breakneck, paradigm-busting speed, Hutchinson takes his time to meander, always purposefully, from antiquity to the present day, often via a strategy of hypotaxis that would give Proust himself a run for his money. It is a tactic he deploys with wit as well as pragmatism, most notably perhaps in 'The Night Autobiographies of Leopold Dice', where the opening assertion "Not another man to outtalk Leopold Dice" is empirically proven over the ensuing three and a bit pages. As a single sentence, it is both playful and affectionate in its mimicry of a certain character, at a certain hour, "when the overproof rum dries up", whilst being deadly serious as a syntactical stealth operation, that elevates what might be dismissed as the merely 'anecdotal' to a larger, diasporic testament that recounts Jamaica's political fissures and positions the Caribbean centre stage. It is this type of procedure, coupled with a referential sweep that encircles Venice via Belarus; Socrates via Seferis; Chaucer alongside Frederick Douglass; together with a swathe of awards and publication by Faber, which has positioned Hutchinson as heir apparent to Derek Walcott.

That said, it would be a shame to read the work outside of its own generational milieux, which would include work by poets such as Malika Booker, Vahni Capildeo and Kei Miller; all of whom, quite distinctly, are engaged in the project of (re)mapping the region in its myriad diversities. Or to omit to note that there are moments of hypnotic lyricism that evoke Louise Glück, in their tone of declarative, spiritual authority:

A soft light, God's idleness
warms the skin of the lake.

[...]

What is terrifying about happiness?
Happiness. The water does not move.

('Small Fantasia: Light Years')

God, as one might expect from a book set predominantly in a country which, according to the *Guinness Book of World Records*, has more churches per square mile than any other nation, is never far away. In 'The Ark by "Scratch"', the intergalactic idiosyncracies of its speaker, reggae producer Lee 'Scratch' Perry, and the cadences of the Old Testament are interwoven with unerring and exhilarating accuracy:

> The genie says build a studio. I build
> a studio from ash. I make it out of peril and slum
> things. [...]

> I credit not the genie but the coral rock: I man am stone.
> I am perfect. Myself is a vanishing conch shell speeding round
> a discothèque at the embassy of angels [...]

And if the ministrations of Scratch are not enough, Hutchinson also refers us to 'Sibelius and Marley', wherein he articulates the lyric's capacity as subversive agent: "History", he writes, "is dismantled music" but, the poem concludes, it is music that "dismantles history".

Karen McCarthy Woolf's latest collection is Seasonal Disturbances *(Carcanet, 2017).*

HOOTS AND MUTTERS

Jackie Kay, Bantams, *Picador, £9.99, ISBN 9781509863174*
Miles Burrows, Waiting for the Nightingale, *Carcanet, £9.99,*
ISBN 9781784103408
Leontia Flynn, The Radio, *Cape, £10, ISBN 9781787330085*

Carol Rumens considers the influence of the oral tradition across
three collections

. . .

Poetry's oral traditions invigorate the work of these three-generation-spanning poets. But for one of them, Jackie Kay, a seeming transition to spoken-word poet has left rather thin pickings for the page.

I would probably enjoy listening to Kay perform much of the work in *Bantam*. It belongs to the glow of her generous personality and voice. She is a gifted performer. Performance poets often blend personal sincerity and learned presentation skills to transport audiences out of a sceptical or listless response; they may speak for a community, especially if they have an official role, like Kay's in Scotland, as national laureate. Originality isn't the first requirement, but the poet-performer must be able to reinvigorate popular tropes, rhymed and otherwise, make us foreground politics over aesthetic scruples, uncurl our toes.

Bantam demonstrates the aesthetic problems besetting the commercial drive to fuse public and private arts. Too many lines falter into doggerel, the rhymes banal, rhyme-schemes erratic, repetitions a heart-tug device that's less compelling than emotionally wearing. Spoken-word customisation is not the only difficulty: some of the poems were commissioned as text, and their 'occasional' character, in the absence of the context, shows up as thinness and vagueness – 'Lines for Kilmarnock', for example, written "for the new war memorial in Kilmarnock". It begins

> Between the lines of men,
> The lines of women come:
>
> In case you think me strange,
> Your postscript never came.
>
> The lines you repeat before you fall
> Into line, and the ones you say when you fall
>
> Asleep.

The first couplet is promising, in its blunt denotive way, but the ensuing non-sequiturs and clunky repetands spell car crash. These must be among the most uninviting lines ever to open a poetry collection. There are further glitches throughout the poem: suffice to say that it was poor editing to have included this one at all, let alone to have given it the opening spot.

Of a handful of poems worthy of Jackie Kay's talents, I enjoyed the reported-speech of the title poem, in which the poet's veteran-father remembers his regiment of "wee men / named efter / sma' chickens", although it must be said that the dialect poems are as uninterested in originality as the rest. Kay has a good ear for voices, and the African asylum-seeker's monologue 'Push the Week' is enlivened by food-stuff names and tangible, sore-stomach hunger, while 'Beech Road Park' is a love-song with moments of Burns-like simplicity and directness: "O but how the leaves have gone this year; / And the trees are suddenly bare. / I walk through Beech Road Park, my dear. / I thought I saw you but you were not there".

Miles Burrows from Leicester is the most joyously inventive comic writer since a certain brilliant Irish Miles (na gCopaleen, aka Flann O'Brien) made his indelible mark. *Waiting for the Nightingale* is Burrows's second collection, published some fifty years after *A Vulture's Egg*, his first. A much-travelled poet-doctor, he brings finesse, imagination and a fierce sense of humour to his work, synchronising the arts of comedy, story-telling and verse-making to remind us there's a craft fundamental to all three – the craft of timing. When poems honour language and narrative, they honour moments of silence, too.

The approach is often Pythonesque, a deadpan narrator packing incongruities together in one bundle and standing calmly back to watch them combust, or dance away somewhere else altogether. While the satire is good-humoured, the eroticism self-mocking, a few sparks may tickle and burn sensitive skin. Burrows laughs at poets and their fond illusions and earnest fetishes, at public-school rituals and mad teachers, at perplexing parents and girlfriends, at the timidity and bravado of the male psyche, at the psychiatric profession, at something we might loosely call 'Englishness'. But wait: his parody of Wallace Stevens, 'Wallace in Undieland', is a strong candidate for the nightingale's tour de force:

> Louche lingeries of logic! Beige on beige
> Philosophies the texture of brioche
> Hold with faint exhalations Marimonde
> Who walks parterres of velvet, pondering
> And longs for vaguer jabots, looser tulle.

At heart, Burrows is a serious critic whose poetry searches souls, its own and ours.

He handles rhyme and para-rhyme with panache, but "Rhyme is no more needed than a two-tone doorbell" he writes in 'English Provincial Poetry', a kind of spoof creative-writing handbook:

> [...] having decided theme and shape,
> Get hold of your objective correlative (see glossary page 47).
> This could be a sunset, often a wild bird (e.g. a hawk, perhaps lame)
> Or some obsolescent piece of country apparatus, such as a spade,
> A dibber (perhaps belonging to your old father) preferably with some
>   nostalgic flavour.
> Old carpentry tools can often be found in car boot sales.

Burrows's poems cross boundaries, blend genres. The best words pursue each other in the best order and yet lift as breath and voice and tone from the page. Performance would suit them. I'm amazed the collection hasn't been decked with prizes. Perhaps the "nightingale" of the title, combined with the Victorian jacket illustration (James Arthur O'Connor's *Moonlight*), is the problem. It may extend the jokes about "moon therapy" and bird-poetry, but the subfusc exterior offers little clue to the sparkling originality within.

Leontia Flynn enjoys a joke, too, but prioritises structure in her fourth collection. The first section, with its textbook-mocking title, 'The Child, The Family', is powerfully focused on the feminine, tracing fragmented contemporary experience into the further disorientations of traditional motherhood.

In the title sequence Flynn inherits some heirlooms from the House of Northern Irish Poetry, but if Heaney's childhood wireless faintly intones the shipping forecast at the start, Flynn swiftly flicks the dial to a grimmer, more desiccated frequency:

> The radio hoots and mutters, hoots and mutters
> out of the dark, each morning of my childhood.
> A kind of plaintive, reedy, oboe note –
> Deadlock...it mutters, firearms...Warrenpoint;
> *Just before two this morning...talks between...*
> ('The Radio')

A more conversational tone emerges with the introduction of the mother:

> [...] small, freaked out, pragmatic, vigilant;
> she's high-pitched and steely – like, in human form,
> the RKO transmitter tower, glimpsed
> just before films on Sunday afternoons,
> where we loaf on poufs, or wet bank holidays.

Flynn, you feel, quietly relishes the class comedy of a once socially mobile word like "pouf", the zeugma of "poufs, or wet bank holidays". Satire nevertheless keeps its distance: the focus is on the small, brave, frayed mother, "steeled" in a war-zone which extends to the child-filled family house, where she "wrangles her youngsters into one bright room / and tries to resist their centripetal force // as she tries to resist the harrowing radio". Five-line stanzaic units, three to a poem, keep everything together in a sequence bookended by a pair of quintains, aubade and epilogue, the latter perfectly concluding "And because I was just a child and understood / nothing at all, I simply fell asleep."

Comedy and poetry meet on a number of occasions, from the hilarious 'The Brunties (an elegy)' to the rather surreal eclogues at the end of the collection, where strangely named allegorical figures, such as "Mother of Older Child, Imploded" and "The Awesome Voice of the Internet" debate with or across each other, occupying a zone between natural speech, philosophy and ornament. Flynn, like Burrows, can be LOL funny. The work of both writers suggests that a primary duty of contemporary poetic intelligence might be to learn to laugh at itself.

Carol Rumens's most recent collection is Perhaps Bag *(Sheep Meadow Press, 2017).*

CALLING OUT THE BEAST

Irene Solà, Beast, *trans. Oscar Holloway and Irene Solà, Shearsman,*
£9.95, ISBN 9781848615526
Shivanee Ramlochan, Everyone Knows I Am a Haunting, *Peepal*
Tree, £8.99, ISBN 9781845233631
Khairani Barokka, Rope, *Nine Arches, £9.99, ISBN 9781911027232*

So Mayer explores a feminine poetics haunted by the spectre of
colonial masculinity

. . .

Beast – *Rope* – *Everyone Knows I Am a Haunting*: the titles of these
three first UK collections knowingly scream/shudder B-movie,
highlighting that the Gothic gurlesque has become a transnational language
for a new *écriture féminine*. As early as 2010, Lara Glenum, writing for
Jacket, highlighted the Goth(ic) elements of the gurlesque, drawing a
genealogy back, via Kathy Acker, to "original Goth girl" Emily Dickinson
– and in these collections, it is as often a writing on the body as of it.

  Cuts, wounds, scabs, births, rapes, abortions, possession, pollution,
drowning: these slim collections are 'Epicdermis', as Khairani Barokka
titles a poem. They iterate litanies of violence that sometimes reach ecstasy,
edging – however self-reflexively – into hysteria. At their best, as in
'Epicdermis', where Okka queries that tired trope, "the analogy of woman
to country... / Colonise at will, with reliable prophylactics", these poems

question and re-vision the spectacularisation, objectification and destruction of bodies identified as female, feminine or feminised, which occurs in language and across the poetic canon as well as in lived experience.

Sometimes, however, these poets' intelligence, awareness of the traditions in which they write, and vivid flexion of language is not a reliable prophylactic against abjection and abstraction, which reproduces the violence it tries to make apparent. What Linda Hutcheon called "complicitous critique", in *The Politics of Postmodernism* (1989), is still relevant and operational. Irene Solà's *Beast* (which offers bilingual English–Catalan texts) struggles hardest (in the dual sense of trying and failing) to exit complicity: the opening epigraph from Sylvia Plath, one that perpetuates the hysterical image of the poet that Jacqueline Rose critiqued in *The Haunting of Sylvia Plath* (1991), sets the tone. Solà (translating into English with Oscar Holloway) writes:

My head between my shoulders
every morning
at a distance from the oven
calms my father,
whose beard and tongue are blue,
and who smiles thinking we don't own a garage.
All these secrets make the girls strange.

('My head between my shoulders')

The references to Plath are self-evident (the oven, the father), along with the favoured Gothic trope of Bluebeard. But the final line implies a fetishisation of being one of Bluebeard's wives, rather than any critique or resistance: as the compact poems tantalise – or even seduce – with half-articulated images of sexual violence, it seems evident that it is the effort of keeping the secret that makes the girls strange. "I don't fancy coming to the couch", Solà writes in the previous poem ('You're always biting me'): in Catalan, the final word is "*sofà*", an echo of the poet's name; the English translation chooses instead the blunt resonance with psychoanalysis.

"I opened [my eyes] wider, / for you to see them better" ('In the OpenCor the fluorescent lights'): the performance of sacrificial, spectacularised femininity – which is seen rather than seeing – has to be somewhat self-aware, in that echo of Red Riding Hood; but it is also end-stopped, the performative offering no alternative. While the title of one poem nods to

Peter Pan, there is barely critique in a final line that refers to making "out of indians, sausages" ('MRS. DARLING') – only complicity. It's hard to hear any irony in this wholesale purchase of the Gothic.

Certainly, the postcolonial poetics of Okka and Shivanee Ramlochan offer a (perhaps, necessarily) more critical stance towards violated bodies and places. Ramlochan, an experienced literary critic and editor, pours her erudition of multiple literatures and spiritual traditions into her dense, long-lined poems. They are poems of productive confusion, where genders, pronouns, religions and myths merge in the body of each poem's speaker, who is comfortably, wilfully multiple. Ramlochan's is an invocatory poetry; the first poem, 'A Nursery of Gods for My Half-White Child', calls on Ganesh, Kali, Shiva, Krishna and Saraswati, saying "some names come before your mother's". The poems wrestle with the overwhelming power of the divine (and the) feminine: when the gods return, in the penultimate poem 'Vivek Considers the Nature of Secrets', Krishna becomes Vivek's rough lover.

As Ramlochan notes in a poem earlier in this third section, 'Camp Burn Down', going "cock to cock to cheap vaseline" remains "unlawful from here [the poet is based in Trinidad] to Tobago and back", and her bold inscription of male–male desire is salutary and welcome. Yet the trace of fire in the poem leads back to an earlier pair, 'Fire, Fire' and 'The Abortionist's Granddaughter Gives Blood', in which a wife and a husband, respectively, each consume the other. The bold figuration of confident male–male relationships operates as performative proxy for surviving the disaster of heteronormativity.

In between the opening section that includes 'Fire, Fire' and the closing section that ends with Vivek is the litany of 'The Red Thread Cycle', seven poems that explore rape culture, moving from abjection to a reclamation of the body and voice through poetry. The red thread that the subject of the first poem carries in her lap becomes a series of references to sewing; in 'IV. The Policeman in Your Throat', "stitch" echoes in "He pitches you open". The work of reparation is undone by the internalisation of dominance, so that the conclusion in 'VII: The Open Mic of Every Deya, Burning', that "Each line break bursts me open / for applause" remains painful, even violating, in its repetition of the act of opening.

Ramlochan's poetry is, appositely, an art of opening: her first lines – such as that poem's "I took to the stage, knifed in" – are incisive, compelling. Elsewhere in the poems, touches of hysteria – "Macbeth for the tropics"

('I: On the Third Anniversary of the Rape') – threaten melodrama. "Blast the bolted doors into hell's abattoir", the final line of 'II. Nail It to the Barn Door Where It Happened', is a far less heart-stopping invocation for the rape survivor than "Make love to yourself in the darkness, in any way you can bear it", which appears midway through.

In a more pragmatic moment, one of Ramlochan's speakers invokes a grandmother for whom "The world can't end when there are animals left to feed" ('Song of the Only Surviving Grandmother'), and it is in such a grounded, multispecies world that many of Okka's poems set their tales. The least narrative poet of those under review, she divides her collection into three, but it is really two: the final section 'Tigo, Telu, Ink on Palm' channels Gertrude Stein's *Tender Buttons* in a series of poems (mixing prose and lyric forms) that fuse and confuse objects and *objets d'art*, some of which have been exhibited as paintings by the poet, who is also a visual artist. The previous two sections both take up themes of immersion in water and impregnation, linked by a concern with climate change and extreme weather events that threaten the delicate ecosystems of the poems.

In 'Steel, Yourself', the New York subway becomes a site of drowning. Although Okka writes that there is "no place / where purity lies / without danger", it is not to invoke or hystericise Romantic or fundamentalist – or even conservationist – purities under threat. In another poem, 'Meteorology', she writes:

In summer,
I am your purple-and-soot
[...]
Epidermis mixed with creamed potatoes, Turkish bread.

Confident in her multitudinous, powerful and mobile existence as the world's weather, the poem's speaker challenges expectations of women of colour. In 'October/April', the speaker reflects on falling into tourist attitudes in (writing about) Nepal, querying whether her poem is "the stealing of a memory from all that is continuous". This poem, and the two that follow, stand out from the rest of the collection for their specificity of place and sense of a world outside the poet's embedding in her embodiment. The very specific, and troubled, seas they present are in unresolved tension with the seas where speakers swim in other poems.

"Tie the rope of yourself to the sea", urges the penultimate poem, bilingually ('Sungai Di Pesisir/River on the Shore'), but in the title poem, which closes the collection, the rope – "something to unknot" – gets tied up with the minotaur, who appears amid Ramlochan's "red thread", too. There is a pervasive mythos of violent, colonial masculinity that these poets cannot (yet) unknot; at least Okka and Ramlochan are calling out the beast.

So Mayer is the author of (O) *(Arc, 2015). A chapbook,* jacked a kaddish, *is forthcoming from Litmus Publishing.*

SHIMMERY ALIEN SYMPATHIES

Stephanie Burt, Advice from the Lights, *Graywolf, $16,*
ISBN 9781555977894
Ahren Warner, Hello. Your Promise Has Been Extracted, *Bloodaxe,*
£12, ISBN 9781780373782

Vidyan Ravinthiran on likeability and unlikeability

. . .

You're not meant to be good at two things, or at being two people: it aggravates those who'd rather stick you in a box. Stephanie Burt (the book appears under her previous name, Stephen) is not only the world's most read, and influential, poetry critic – she's an original in verse too. Poet-critics (a dying breed?) can be tribal. They know what they like, and it resembles them – verse which wears their smell. Burt's different. She likes lots of things, and not in a transiently peppy, wanting-to-be-friends-with-everybody sort of way. 'Fairy Story Stephanie' has been there, done that:

> Until recently
> I could not tell any difference
> between "I want to meet people like me,"
> "I want people to like me,"
> and "I want to go out of my way to meet people like me

except that I want there to be nobody like me,
only a mirror in air
and a series of shimmery alien sympathies.

Recently, I asked another poet which poets he admired. He paused, and said: "Well, there are the three of us here at this table…" Eye roll: I'm with Burt on this one. Our subculture can only survive (I speak of poetry, and poets, though I'm tempted to talk politics) if we're ready to be impressed, pleasured, disturbed, and transformed by those who don't look like us, or write like us, read like us, or smell like us; who – shock horror – we might never even have met.

Advice from the Lights includes poems about being a child; others evoke an imagined, girl-bodied adolescence; Burt's verse speaks, too, on behalf of sundry objects and animals. These poems resemble Marianne Moore's, a bit, bending the inhuman towards the human: 'To the Naked Mole Rats at the National Zoo', for one, though Burt quotes prurient grade-schoolers, and not the esoteric sources Moore prefers: "One compared you to severed toes. / Another called all of you "skin tubes," which seems apropos, / if rude." Slant-rhymes suit poems in which no one and nothing is only what it is, and where what we like to think of as a solidly persisting self is in fact confected on the hoof:

All the colors I recognize are alive
in the pebbles at the bottom of my tank.
I pretend each trace or trail
I make in the clarified water
amounts to my emphatic signature,
which I have chosen to leave in invisible ink.

('Scarlet: A Betta')

Burt's poems bring others to mind: Michael Hofmann ('My bedtime and I were both eight' has his cauterised viciousness), and A.K. Ramanujan ('Water Strider'). But these aren't weaknesses: we're all a congeries of echoes, and suppressing or disguising an inheritance may be the cowardly, the easier, option.

Burt has an ear for a punchline. 'Secondhand Flashlight': "I have no say / over who or what turns me on". 'Fifth Grade Time Capsule': "The people who pick me up can never be / the same as the ones who put me down".

Other poems are earnestly self-revealing – we recognise the tonalities (from blogs, social media, talk-shows, the kind of wonderful late-night conversations which shatter proprieties): "I'm so afraid / of a grand faux pas that I answer the most banal // questions by quoting the questioner, so as to let / his words shield mine" ('Roly-Poly Bug'). Burt – as reviewer, as poet – reveals the origin of confidence in an aboriginal disquiet. The most compelling sentences (the kind written not just by novelists, but also elite critics) are made of stammers.

The best, deepest poem in this fizzy, nervous, compelling book must be 'Concord Grapes', which, to begin with, sounds like one of Burt's essays:

> What would it be like to belong
> entirely in your own body, or in your own country, or at
> your own address? It might
> be like these unselfconscious, tangled, each-
> one-over-the-next-one Concord grapes,
> hooked (as in hook-and-eye) on the chain-link fence
> between our driveway and the next;
> the populous dewy clusters
> hang as if lashed
> to so many miniscule masts,
> or threaded and caught in the stems of their earnest
> commensals and competitors.

Something happens in the fourth line. The critic's prose intelligence – posing a question, mobilising the reader's curiosity – gives way to a straggly acknowledgment of what simply surrounds her (slant-rhymes, again, provide a scaffold: "lashed", "masts", "earnest".) We're reminded of Odysseus, persevering past the sirens; there's violence, here, too (prisoners, slaves, lashed by their masters?), drifting into economics. *Commensal*: the word describes a relationship of mutual if unconscious benefit between two organisms. (The root phrase is Latin, it means to eat at the same table.) The poem explains that grapes can only thrive if they're "consumed" – that is, if people want to eat and drink them – touching on the trampling of them as a revolutionary image; in a grisly teleportation-act, the reader meets suddenly "the scavenger-mutilated / or putrefying corpses of Shiloh / and Andersonville". It occurs to me – reading this poem, enthralled by its gambits – that what I admire in Burt's verse is the pressure, self-applied, from line to line, to say something interesting to, and acknowledging of, as many people as possible.

Ahren Warner's new poems, some in prose, mingle with photographs. These are suggestively washed-out, they depict dilapidation, and the print quality is excellent. Warner's verse appears to discuss this collocation of scarified surfaces – their bitty, cracked, granular noise, redolent of industrial disuse, and abuse – with the hygienic space in which art is consumed:

> According to Kristeva's *Strangers to Ourselves*, the community can be defined as *a set that, by definition, comes into being by excluding the dissimilar*. As I rewrite this, from an armchair in Parmentier, hundreds are drowning off the shores of Athens, of Marseille, of Sicily and Almeria.

> In Almeria, prostitutes whose bones jut like those of death-camp Jews, prostitutes with slash-scars from hip to hip, fellate and fuck for cash or junk. I know this because, in a small gallery east of Baixa, a man receives an award for their portraits.

For Warner, poetry is a serious thing, and says serious things, but this seriousness has to be recovered from a media triviality which we can't simply ignore (that would be cheating). I can't say literary theory excites me as it does him, and I've been wrongfooted in the past by his mixtures of po-mo self-awareness with a rush to gravitas – it might have to do with proximity rather than distance, my attraction to the same ingredients, but in other quantities.

But this is poetry (it *is* poetry) of extraordinary poise and power. The final sentence of each shaped paragraph isn't as resigned as you think – the poet doesn't throw his hands up – there persists the possibility of resistance, in the teeth of global distraction. Warner's disgust is salutary, if terminal (I don't know where he'll go from here). This isn't a pleasant book to read, though Warner's phrasing is always honed, with an exquisiteness to the placing of sounds that can also be read as urgency. Maybe the photographs preserve a quantum of transcendence? Tender-seeming, that is, pink, flesh-toned, paint flakes eerily from a wall. Craquelure. Or, a *gash*, to quote the poet:

I am neither particularly tall, nor remotely narrow, nor gifted at small talk or brief, meaningful encounters.

This, perhaps, is one of the reasons that I find myself moved by the shimmy from rage to tears of a man in a café, here, on Eratosthenous.

Fuck the Germans
– his voice is a gash.

[...]

In truth, I am not particularly shocked by this man's animosity towards a country that friends of mine call home. A country in which I am often at home.

I am preoccupied with the fact of this man: a man who has served me coffee every day for a week, a man for whom I have no name.

Here is a politics of social interaction – its failures – attentive to atrocities, Warner pursues his analysis down to the tiniest molecule of stalled amiability ("*Often* at home"!) An everyday encounter stands, in microcosm, for large, nationwide, global, failures of empathy.

Warner touches you through the ear and through the eye. His conceptual forays are ergonomically grooved, and stippled, and pitted (you can hold onto these ideas), by an understated melopoeia, and his ability to shock, of a sudden, with a noticed detail. The poet (it's usually a man) with aspirations to be *major*, has a way of turning punitive, of disavowing the very art form he practises, to achieve a position of unassailable authority; power-worship may be disguised as realism, and self-regard as historical awareness, gemmed with raindrops of value (those "brief, meaningful encounters" which suffice for some). Such is the road Warner's on, and he knows it, and he knows that you know. But he can write so well: there's no one I'd rather be appalled by.

Vidyan Ravinthiran is the author of Grun-tu-molani *(Bloodaxe, 2014) and* Elizabeth Bishop's Prosaic *(Bucknell University Press, 2015).*

FULL OF SOUL

Jacqueline Saphra, All My Mad Mothers, *Nine Arches*, £9.99,
ISBN 9781911027201
Roddy Lumsden, So Glad I'm Me, *Bloodaxe*, £9.95,
ISBN 9781780373706

Rory Waterman on unreliable narratives and musical inspirations

. . .

The first two sections of Jacqueline Saphra's second full-length collection, respectively focused on young childhood and adolescence, constitute a sort of fractured coming-of-age narrative in the past tense. The poems are by turns sentimental and hardened about what seems at once a dysfunctional and loving upbringing for its narrator. In the prose poem 'Getting into Trouble', for example,

> My boyfriend, who was stupid but useful, told all his friends I was a virgin and forced me to see *Close Encounters of the Third Kind* three times and listen to nothing but Genesis, which I preferred to The Sex Pistols, because I never believed there was No Future, not when my mother was, at least for now, empty-wombed and full of soul, as she stirred a pot of her famous lentil soup, not yet tied by blood to the man she loved.

The poems' narratives are sometimes unreliable enough for us to have to do some work to see where the values lie. The title poem presents one woman in multiple guises, some apparently more literal than others, none allowing us to see her whole:

> My mother barely spoke between her bruises:
> her low-cut gown was tea-stained silk, and from behind
> her Guccis or Versaces, she would serve us salty dinners,
> stroke a passing cheek, or lay her head on any waiting shoulder.
>
> [...]
>
> My mother was so hard to grasp: once we found her
> in a bath of extra virgin olive oil, her skin well slicked.
> She'd stocked the fridge with lard and suet, butter – salted
> and unsalted – to ease her way into this world. Or out of it.

The book's breathless opening poem has given this some context. It presents a mother (there is nothing in the poems to suggest it isn't the same woman, though also no indication of how much or what is true) gathering her baby into a car bought by the child's father, and ending up on the roundabout at Hyde Park Corner, "not sure how to execute the move outwards". It would be a superb metaphor for escape succumbing to psychological entrapment if Saphra didn't then explain it away by telling us she had never been "properly taught how to make an exit".

Some of the poems are straightforwardly marvellous, though – such as the acutely observed, moving and witty 'Mile End', which ends, also symbolically, with "one hand / on my cheek, one hand on my hand"; or 'Things We Can't Untie', the sort of poem destroyed by paraphrasing, which is as moving and clinical as any poem of youthful trauma I can recall. The risk of her style is that others, such as 'Volunteers, 1978' simply don't quite do enough to transcend anecdote. The speaker, it seems, was working on a kibbutz, where "The new girls did the bloody work, / chopping the heads off but saving / the necks", and "I went right off chicken".

The third section generally finds the speaker (for the collection has one consistent voice) in domesticated adulthood. Occasionally, the poems cleverly pick up strands dropped earlier in the book. 'Chicken', a few pages beyond 'Volunteers, 1978', ends with a daughter's jaded, youthful belligerence: "If you choose to eat an animal, / you must first learn to kill it, / my daughter told me / as I snipped the plastic film". The fourth and final section then brings the book into the present tense with a disparate cluster of pieces, some meditative and others less so. 'Spunk', an ekphrastic sonnet about Jacob Epstein's *Adam* (look that up now if you don't know it) takes something of a wry and less androcentric slant on the origin myth:

> Drunk on lust, pumped up with blood, he stands
> broad on his plinth and howls for cunt. Who'd dare
> to leave that call unanswered? This is where
> we find the source: that first, primeval sin:
> he forced an opening, she let him in.

And towards the very end, there are poems considering love in (relative) age, and simultaneously looking back and taking stock, as in the pitch-perfect 'Everlasting': "Sometimes at night, I lie with all my dead beside me / in the absolute dark". There is a fair amount of little consequence in this book, but its high points are variously touching, cajoling, witty and, on occasion, immaculate. Saphra is a fine poet, with plenty to say, who eschews any hint of dogmatism, and she has written a book that is apparently personal but which never gazes at its navel.

Roddy Lumsden's tenth collection is another book of four parts: 'Till it Runs Clear', 'A Soft Leviathan', 'With All of Your Might', and 'Kippers and Glitter'. In the opening poem, 'Simone's Cookie', he writes, "I'm thinking about everything", and that would pass as a more practical, perfunctory title: few collections cover as much ground as this, or seem to reveal such a lithe and obsessive mind.

The cover displays a photograph of Sandy Denny, lead singer of Fairport Convention. If you've never heard of her, you are perhaps especially likely to struggle with the middle two sections, dominated by what are dubbed 'conflation poems' in which, as the blurb puts it, Lumsden has "knocked the square peg of one subject through the round hole of another – often music-related". 'Coldplay/Foreplay', like most others, brings musical allusions into an anecdote – here beginning with a woman apparently masturbating to Coldplay, as one does: "Amber Eyes has pulled her top up to her neck / and her hands are down her barely-there shorts. / She's on the floor. She is blaring out 'Clocks'". By the end, "I will jump ship and join her, / and you can guess where my hands will go". Down your barely-there shorts?

'Amber Eyes' is the human subject throughout the second section, including the joyously odd 'Back-up Flats':

> Amber Eyes is trying out her stilettos,
> Criss-crossing the seagrass rug. She
> Is brushing up for Beating Retreat,
> The annual military ceremony in town.
> Music? Anything but Snow Patrol,
> I tell her and she plays a full hour
> Of Chopin.

This is all very readable in its way, but the ultimate feeling is of wasting time rather than filling it. The third section of the book cuts deeper in places, but is equally allusive – and, at times, equally happy to embrace a febrile version of the male gaze. 'In Bath with Madonna' finds the speaker and Queen of Pop soaking and small-talking to post-rock chamber music: "We are awkward and listening to Rachel's, / the Music for Egon Schiele album. We fit, / just about. Of course, we play with soap / and eye each other."

Though billed on its dust jacket as Lumsden's "most optimistic and accessible book since *The Book of Love*" (his second collection, published in 2000), it is frequently neither. Many of the poems heap impression on top of impression in a manner that is simultaneously chatty and inscrutable. 'Passing Pond Road' begins: "The demons give us symmetry, ducks synching / on the Princess pond, couple with prammed twins, / yoghurt which pretends but is a gluey composure / of diabolic symmetry. Swing door mood." The poem in fact reaches towards a portentous concluding epiphany about our inherent need for 'duality' and oneness: "We climb / to each other, aching a little, then, rocked to rest, / yearning so blithely to be that impossible – one". A part-complementary, part-contradictory sentiment is at the heart of 'Simone's Carouself': "Then shirk the us. Us being the downtime / of the self. I need alone". But such poems, quantum-leaping between staccato images and sentences, can be painfully difficult to unpack. Others are perhaps too straightforward, but don't get us far. 'Twenty-four Hours of People Saying Nope' is nearly fifty lines of sentences that might be moved around with no obviously deleterious effect:

> Nope declares Faycal, everyone talks
> to themselves and they are lying if they

say they don't. Nope says Calum, quietly,
the shop will not be open at this hour.

"I do promise / to stop this listing", he writes in 'Tending to the Reliable', and his poems are often more effective when he does. Others turn a choppy, compressed style to fine effect, though, such as 'Work Crush', which marries Lumsden's slaloming style to a scenario that feels like Arab Strap channelling David Brent: "Deborah, her sweater blooming, bites / her bottom lip and all the hormones trip. [...] I have nothing, nothing / this evening but telly and ready meal".

Among those "optimistic and accessible" poems is a little masterpiece, the quiet, vivid 'The Hoopoe', set in Barcelona: "there it is: // a hoopoe on a branch. 'A hoopee?' she says. / Hoopee. I go sweet for this still on anxious days". Then: "one night a month on, she wakes me: // 'I liked the hoopee,' talking in her sleep. / Which is all the answer I will ever need". This is vulnerable, hearty, alert to what we should most treasure. And even in its less successful moments, this is a book of considerable humanity.

Rory Waterman's latest publication is Sarajevo Roses *(Carcanet, 2017).*

LOOKING FOR HER ROOTS

Sasha Dugdale, Joy, *Carcanet, £9.99,* ISBN *9781784105037*
Sina Queyras, My Ariel, *Coach House, $19.95,* ISBN *9781552453544*

Claire Crowther on mothers and foremothers, and the endurance
of history and myth

· · ·

J oy, Dugdale's fourth collection (excluding translations) and a 2017
Poetry Book Society Choice, escorts the reader courteously and
quietly through displacements, disavowals and the destructive forces of
history. Here are lines from 'How my friend went to look for her roots':

> This little town had an ancient centre, but nowhere to eat. The
> little hotel was shut for repairs a thousand years
> in the completing, and the woman who poked her head from a
> window said:
>
> –If you're from here then why don't you stay with your family?
>
> –My family left.
>
> So, asked the woman, why come here then?

Fable is where facts start as well as end, *Joy* suggests, as here with its echo of Rip Van Winkle. 'The Canoe', about the making of local fables, could be an oral poem delivered on an Anglo-Saxon winter's night: loved community members have sailed away, those left behind have become resentful and destroyed the empty homes of their lost members:

> So who can blame the ones who broke in and stole
> Who brought on the collapse, by breaking in doors and windows
> Who fell about in a wild frenzy then, and drove at ceilings, boards
> With hooked poles, hoping for treasures to come pouring forth.
> Then, encouraged by the fierce and glorious joy of destruction
> They cudgelled chairs with chair legs, tossed cups like coconuts
> Stamped and urinated and spat at the walls in spasms

Such near-biblical lines, in this long free-verse poem declaimed by a wise bard, help convey our myth of dispersal through war as well as in travel and language. Forced displacements are framed in other familiar styles. Ballad, sonnet, villanelle lull the reader into facing horror. Dugdale leaps geographic and historic distances to give moral perspective, even using human size, as in 'Ironing the Spider', a poem whose title echoes its irony. "My most violent act: once ironing a spider," says the narrator, adding "I can't abide violence." Subsequently, the "large" spider rears up, a "meaty widow":

> I have since seen her soul all scorched and resentful
> Her spirit crushed and oozing. I am reminded then
> Of the railway victims on the Pskov station board.
> It read: do you recognize these men?
>
> [...]
>
> I knew them all. We were of the same species
> Not *sapiens* perhaps, but *homo* for sure
> I could have ironed their shirts, their sheets,
> Sat waiting for them, cross-legged on the kitchen floor.

Dugdale's unruffled tone makes the gendered thrust of historic victimhood more piercing. The long title poem, winner of the Forward Prize for Best Single Poem in 2016, is a nuanced feminist depiction of Catherine Blake, wife and co-artist to William Blake:

I remember how you taught me many things. When I met you a
thousand years ago and that is not extravagant because you knew
how to press on time and release it from its skin to grow you knew
that about time and all manner of other wisdoms and how to release
the sky from the indignant thistle, and colour from powder and line
from copper and sense from letters which danced like demons on
the page.

It's an intense lyrical outpouring from a woman close to death and
compelling drama too – Dugdale is a successful dramatist and casts many
believable voices throughout the book. But here's the strange thing about
this collection: because it's mostly plain and simple in style, its eerily odd
quality here and there stands out, like an original text lurking behind a
translation. Dugdale edited *Modern Poetry in Translation* for five years and
her own translations, Chekhov's *The Cherry Orchard* for example, show an
excellent command of idiom. *Joy* has occasional aberrancies. Full stops
are used but not systematically, and there's a slightly uncomfortable feel
to some phrases and lines, as in this hard-to-read syntax in 'Valentine's':

Irritability, like the substance left by vapours
That have long departed the alembic's lung
And taste with a quetsch's bitter tongue.

Or this in 'The Canoe': "They could not bear a thing dispossessed, a thing
un-useful. / The spare goods made them chafe and grieve, from there to
thieve."

Defamiliarisation is a poetic style promoted by early twentieth-century
Russian poets as Dugdale, who lived in Russia for five years, will know; it
is a poetic convention today. *Joy* does it more subtly than most. These
compelling stories of strange happenings in an almost imperceptibly
strange style make your mind understand foreignness as our process.
Sasha Dugdale is a wise bard and her book is a civilising read.

Poetry may often be compressed, but the feelings it expresses are not.
Canadian poet Sina Queyras, in her third collection *My Ariel* (referring to
Sylvia Plath's posthumous collection), expands on anger, the characteristic
feeling in Plath's poetry. Here it is in a long poem, 'Years', composed
mainly of quotes from Plath and Plath literature:

                                              Ariel is a burst,
A big fuck you to the corset, why bang back on domesticity's
Door? The poem, the poem, it's not pastoral at all, it's war,
War, war.

My Ariel is confessional in form. Queyras integrates her own life and Plath's life, her own poetry and Plath's poetry, into a thorough examination of how Queyras's vocation as a poet has survived being parented as well as becoming a parent herself:

Babies sleep under my tongue. Quiet now,
I must rest my mind, surround myself
With creamy Amazons, those I have glimpsed
Through strips of tinfoil winking like crows – no,
No, you cannot eat my heart, I have wrapped

My organs, stacked my selves in sleeves
Of muslin: one of me must survive. One of me
Must live on between the lines.
                              ('The Bee Meeting')

At double the length of *Ariel*, *My Ariel* feels overlong: Queyras uses poem after poem from Plath's book, titling them often as Plath did, to describe the guilt, frustration and eventual absolution of parents: how the narrator's mother has killed a child (inadvertently), how Ted Hughes deals with Plath's death for the rest of his life, how the narrator drifts, guilt-fogged, into the male parental role as she is sidelined by her partner giving birth, in these lines from 'In the Birth Canal':

I am not who I thought I would be in this situation. I cannot recog-
      nize myself at all. I am all shortcomings. All lack.
I pace. Wait. Go in search of a vending machine. In the elevator
      there are no forceps. I think, This must be an oversight.
A young man with a mop and pail sits in a corridor filled with
      discarded medical equipment texting and talking by Bluetooth.
Ted was with you for both births. My father caught me. I am observ-
      ing myself observe.

If birth parents are projected as the enemy, poet-forebears must step up, as Harold Bloom has observed in *The Anxiety of Influence* (1973), to be killed off by the offspring they have inspired. Plath, the myth, is unkillable but the struggle shows in the most dynamic section of the book, the last part, an account of the poet's final push not so much away from the dominance of the mother as toward acceptance of her own gender-conflicted parenthood. 'Tribes of Mommies Just Like You' claims writing as the way forward:

> Apparently there are tribes of mommies who think like men and
> tribes of men who think like mommies. Elsewhere there are
> writers who move fluidly through these modes. I am on the
> lookout. I am watching pronouns foam at the wake.

Ending on her own version of 'Ariel' and a positive note of ongoing happy parenthood and poethood – much as Plath's original ordering of *Ariel* ended with 'Wintering', a hopeful poem about spring coming – Queyras acknowledges the strength of all parents, including the female one burgeoning inside Queyras herself:

> My love hauls
>
> Me up. She is still here,
> Beside me. We float on a white
> Sea, Sylvia, where the dead
>
> Make themselves particulars
> That hang together
> And form something firm
>
> As flanks; steps
> Of joy that, like the hours,
> We master and release.

Claire Crowther's latest publication is Bare George (Shearsman, 2016).

A REAL THING THAT HAPPENS

Hera Lindsay Bird, Hera Lindsay Bird, *Penguin, £9.99*,
ISBN 9780141987408
Jenna Clake, Fortune Cookie, *Eyewear, £10.99*,
ISBN 9781911335528
Kaveh Akbar, Calling a Wolf a Wolf, *Penguin, £9.99*,
ISBN 9780141987972

Jane Yeh finds wit, excess and directness in a group of first
collections

. . .

In this unusually varied and accomplished group of debut collections, Hera Lindsay Bird's comes across as the most colloquial and unruly, like a teenager crashing their parents' dinner party. This is largely a good thing, as Bird's comic poems leap off the page, even when they sound lovelorn: "so many nights of watching you recede from me, / like the ass end of a horse / in the credits of a Western". Originally published last year by Victoria University Press in New Zealand, Bird's poems often have a rather goth air, but delivered with a knowing wit – a self-conscious awareness of their own excesses. As she informs us at one point, "The official theme of all my poems ... is / You get in love and then you die!" The colourful ways in which Bird imagines love, death, and not being dead yet grant her work an appealing energy and freshness.

Bird's combination of faux-morbid imagery, deadpan humour, and ironic-but-sincere emoting recalls the gurlesque style of poetry that originated in late-1990s America, particularly the work of Chelsey Minnis (whom Bird name-checks twice in the collection). At her best, Bird can rival her idol's exuberant inventiveness and talent for surprising imagery: "Hate is a white crêpe box, with voluminous spite ruffles". The sparse layout of words in the multi-page poem 'Mirror Traps' resembles that of many Minnis poems, but with white space instead of endless ellipses to separate the words and lines.

> I want to lie alone   &
>   trembling
> in my hot   neural vacancy
>
>
> like a jet shadow
>
>
>   across a distant field of corn

Bird also excels at comedic melodrama, as in this explanation (in 'Hate') of why she hates certain people:

> [...] I was born to feel a great pettiness
> To lie face-down in my catholic schoolgirl outfit
> and pound the cobblestones of the Royal Albert Hall

Perhaps inevitably, the verve of Bird's style sometimes flags over the course of the collection, while a number of poems (earlier work?) fall flat. The oft-cited 'Keats Is Dead So Fuck Me From Behind' and 'Monica' (as in *Friends*), which are probably entertaining in performance, feel one-note on the page. In other poems Bird lapses into generalised pronouncements like "I thought I was mad at you but I was mad at life" ('Everything Is Wrong'), or "I want to talk about return / and how pain can be a place of welcome" ('Daylight Savings'). Weak spots aside, *Hera Lindsay Bird* is a lively and enjoyable debut from a poet whose voice "overcomes you like a luxury blow-wave".

By contrast, the poems in Jenna Clake's *Fortune Cookie* are written in an intentionally affectless tone, one of neutral reportage. This she uses to great effect to create distinctive and unsettling narratives in which strange characters ("the seal boy", "the Dreamers") try, and fail, to find contentment. *Fortune Cookie* consists mainly of prose poems, a form Clake handles with assurance; her deceptively ordinary-looking prose paragraphs conceal worlds of unexplained weirdness.

In 'The Exit', a prose poem in twenty-eight short sections, a nameless protagonist is driving on a motorway with his or her partner; they pick up a hitchhiker who happens to be a red panda named George. Written in an eerie second-person present tense – "You have taken the wrong exit", "You are now driving down narrow lanes" – the poem keeps doubling back on and repeating itself, contradicting its own narrative until it unravels completely. It reads like a perverse Choose Your Own Adventure novel, at once nightmarish and funny: "You are trying not to scream, like you have just eaten lasagne and been told that it actually contains horse". Over the course of the piece, Clake obliquely exposes cracks in the couple's relationship and hints at issues of control and intimacy, but leaves the story unresolved.

A similar aesthetic of indeterminacy is demonstrated by many of the poems in the collection, which depict pairs or groups of characters caught in surreal situations that end very much *in medias res*. Like Rorschach ink blots, Clake's poems leave us alone to interpret their significance, rather than announcing their import. Their deliberate flatness of tone, however, is enlivened by a dry, understated sense of humour. In one poem a long-suffering wife reports, "My husband wears an eye mask to bed. I must guide him with my voice; he moves as though he is trying to pin a tail on me". The book's funniest piece is 'Carapace', an extended tale about a town where everyone seems to keep pet turtles, and the escalating panic that ensues when the turtles suddenly go missing: "Weekly vigils were held / for the lost turtles. We left bowls of our turtles' favourite food outside our front doors". Fights break out between neighbours; the mayor, the WI, and the Working Men's Club get involved; the local police start a hotline in case any missing turtles call in. Clake's sardonic eye for detail renders the preposterous utterly convincing – when people start putting up laminated "turtle missing" posters, "[t]here was a local shortage of laminating pouches and a 23% increase in house fires caused by laminators". Clake juggles satire, social commentary, and a subtly haunting sense of loss throughout the poem, qualities that also permeate *Fortune Cookie* as a whole. Dreamlike yet grounded in reality, crisply deadpan yet playful and imaginative, these narratives of miscommunication manage to suggest the regrets and uncertainties that lurk behind our outward selves.

Published last year in America by an independent press and now available here, Kaveh Akbar's *Calling a Wolf a Wolf* is easily deserving of the advance praise that accompanies it. Akbar's poems are complex and many-layered, rich with images and ideas yet thankfully concise, without the sprawl and bagginess that similarly serious-minded US poets like Jorie Graham favour. What struck me most was the poems' enviably fluent and assured voice, which is embodied in first-person lyrics capable of accommodating numerous changes of direction, movement, thought – the seemingly effortless ability to shift from one idea to another. The 'I' of the poems is meditative, questioning and musing over the past and the world around him, but never po-faced or self-important:

> [...] It's all I can do to quiver
> in and out of my jeans each day, to keep
> my fingers out of the wrong mouths.
> ('Wake Me Up When It's My Birthday')

While sacrificing none of their linguistic and conceptual sophistication, Akbar's poems retain an inviting, direct quality that makes for a compelling read.

The collection's most obvious subject is the author's struggle with alcoholism, rehab, and recovery, which he explores through a mixture of evocative and unexpected imagery and unusual statements. In the title poem: "I try to find small comforts   purple clover growing in the long / grass   a yellow spider on the windowsill   I am less horrible than I could / be".

The series of ten poems titled 'Portrait of the Alcoholic with [X]' – e.g., 'Portrait of the Alcoholic with Home Invader and Housefly', 'Portrait of the Alcoholic Frozen in Block of Ice', etc. – is formally varied and eclectic in content, encompassing many other experiences as well as that of living with addiction. Indeed, the book ranges widely over themes such as love and desire; the body; a modern longing for some kind of religious belief; family and childhood; and Akbar's Iranian heritage:

[...] Sometimes
when I listen to old Persian music
I get so sad I can actually smell rosewater.
This is a Real Thing That Happens.

('The New World')

While the expansiveness of the collection is a bit overwhelming (several poems could have been cut for space), its subjects should also appeal to a breadth of readers.

When Akbar writes,

[...] I am sealing all my faults with platinum

so they'll gleam like the barrel of a laser gun. [...]
[...] Nobody

ever pays me enough attention

('Everything that Moves Is Alive and
a Threat – A Reminder')

it's both tongue-in-cheek and in earnest. The desire for self-improvement as invincibility, the desire for recognition or love that necessitates vulnerability: these are just two of the conflicting urges that Akbar holds in balance in *Calling a Wolf a Wolf*. An impressively sustained work, this collection captures the highs and lows of what it means to be alive, in a body, on this earth – and how to keep surviving it.

Jane Yeh is the author of The Ninjas *(2012) and* Marabou *(2005), both published by Carcanet.*

NATIONAL ANTHEMS

A Blade of Grass: New Palestinian Poetry, *ed. Naomi Foyle,*
Smokestack, £9.99, ISBN 9780995767539

Nahrain Al-Mousawi considers the range of voices in this
translingual anthology

. . .

The lineage of *A Blade of Grass: New Palestinian Poetry* is quite
apparent: the title is picked up from a quote by iconic Palestinian
poet Mahmoud Darwish: "Against barbarity, poetry must stand with
human frailty, like a blade of grass in a wall as armies march by." While
the anthology gestures toward an iconic predecessor, it is composed of a
distinct and contemporary collection of voices. Indeed, the introduction
makes note of these "new and established voices from the Palestinian
territories, the diaspora, and from within the disputed borders of Israel;
women and men [...] bilingual poets who translate their own work and
Palestinian poets who write in English."

Yet the anthology can't resist inviting comparison with its poetic
precursors. Maya Abu Al-Hayyat's 'Insight', written in Arabic and co-
translated by Foyle and herself, recalls the almond blossoms of Darwish's
late poetry. In Darwish's 'To Describe an Almond Blossom' (from his 2005
collection *Almond Blossoms and Beyond,* translated into English by
Mohammad Shaheen in 2009), he lamented wryly,

If a writer were to compose a successful piece
describing the almond blossom, the fog would rise
from the hills, and people, all the people, would say:
This is it.
These are the words of our national anthem.

Abu Al-Hayyat picks up the almond blossoms with the same disdain as
Darwish, as markers of the facile, hollow allure of symbols of endurance,
patriotism, and national resistance, without sustained action:

I am waiting for a brave martyr's daughter
To stand up and scream
Take your homeland
And give me back my dad

The almond blossom knows its life is short
But the bud cracks and yawns
And only when it falls on the streets of the school
Does happiness bloom.

But in Abu Al-Hayyat's poetry these hollow symbols yield something
broader: the fallen petals transform not only into a glib symbol but also a
shattered life and a shattered family, deftly combining the macro- and
micro-elements of occupation and resistance:

All the minutes of silence
Cannot return one voice to life
I've lived a life filled with heroes
And complete bastards
Now I can no longer distinguish between them
I have seen children
Who gave their parents to the homeland
But I have never seen a homeland
That gave an orphan a father.

She recalls the South African writer Njabulo Ndebele's assessment of the
significance of social and cultural practices to national politics – the
privileging of "state-level politics" within "nationalist discourse" to the

neglect of everyday dynamics, like a shattered family, post-martyrdom:

> Politics is not only the seizure of state power, it is also the seizure of
> power in a woman's burial society in a township; it is the seizure of
> family power by children, thus altering drastically the nature of the
> family, something that might have tremendous implications for the
> new society to be born.

But the work of these new poets – to whom the Anglophone world, and
most likely the Arabic-speaking world, has yet to be as well-acquainted as
to Darwish and Fadwa Tuqan – is quite thematically distinct, as a whole.
The impact of globalisation is a trope that winds its way through the
collection. Abu Al-Hayyat's 'Painful Pictures' contemplates the effect of
circulating images of suffering online – which are meant to elicit empathy
yet often desensitise:

> Twenty men
> In old leather coats
> Gamblers in cheap sportswear
> Faces exude beards, pain and cold
> Mouths wrapped in hands and plates and scarves
> Snow falls on everything
> The sentence below reads
> 'Syrians waiting in the cold and rain to buy bread'
> With an invitation to see more photos
> I do not enter
> I'm no saint
> I'm just a bored person
> Who browses painful images
> To cry a little and thank God
> For the blessing of a warm house
> Then put more rags on the window

In the second section, the only line suggests an internet link, making note
of the absurd and automated expectation of shared grief: "For more painful
images please click here."

 The global circulation of imagery and discourse in our technological
age is also evoked by one of the most delightful stylistic innovations in

the anthology – the 'textu' by poet of the diaspora Fady Joudah (also a physician and translator based in Texas). With the "u" in 'textu' echoing that of the haiku, the textu has the 160-character limit of an (old-style) text message. The poems' only formal constraint is shaped by the urgency of communication and its parameters (character limits), yet each word and each line break invites deliberate contemplation.

Another poet of the diaspora, New York-based Farid Bitar, reveals fragments of different languages and histories, as well as imageries of lost geographies. Both the rhythm and lyricality of his work evoke American urban and Palestinian topographies, as he easily moves between Chicago jails and IDF soldiers, between the wrongfully imprisoned Darby Tillis and Gaza invasions, in 'A Pain Never Heals'. A spoken-word artist, Bitar "writes and performs back-and-forth in Arabic and English", and has translated his own poetry for the anthology, revealing the translingual condition of various writers of the diaspora who live and write in a language that is not their mother tongue. But Bitar's translingual poetry and translations are also metaphorically reflective of the work many of the poets in the anthology do: translating the existential and social conditions of Palestinians within the territories and in the diaspora for audiences beyond their circles and communities.

This speaks to the second theme that distinguishes the new Palestinian poetry from its more iconic predecessors: encounters with structures of occupation are a prominent feature, conveying the marked presence of Israeli soldiers, images of checkpoints, verses born of prisons – the looming, omnipresent elements of occupation that have increased over the years in territories to which Palestinians have been relegated. Abu Al-Hayyat again combines the major, radical features of the state with the repetition of the quotidian:

I'm a destitute woman

Who lives on a checkpoint
Trivial things make me happy
As when my day passes without seeing a single bored soldier
I write my new novel there
About the butcher who wanted to become a violinist

Dareen Tatour, the poet infamously imprisoned for her verses in October 2015, and who is still under house arrest, writes a poem from prison on the day of her indictment (the translation is by Tariq Al Haydar):

> See, prison is for lovers.
> I interrogated my soul
> during moments of doubt and distraction:
> 'What of your crime?'
> Its meaning escapes me now.
> I said the thing and
> revealed my thoughts;
> I wrote about the current injustice,
> wishes in ink,
> a poem I wrote...

To the translators' credit, the English versions read smoothly, unencumbered by partiality to the Arabic-writing style, which can often render a translation stylistically awkward and antiquated, compromising its readability. The thematic and formal innovations of this new anthology make it a welcome addition to the body of poetry distinguishing Palestinian tradition but also to the contemporary flow of transnational verse as it translates the thorny nexus between the local, national, and global.

Nahrain Al-Mousawi is a professor of English Literature at the University of Balamand. She currently resides in Lebanon.

THE NATIONAL POETRY COMPETITION 2017

Judges: Hannah Lowe, Andrew McMillan, Pascale Petit

The judges share comments below on the top three winners in the National Poetry Competition 2017 – Dom Bury, Mary Jean Chan and Momtaza Mehri. These poems are published for the first time here. All ten winning poems can be read in the National Poetry Competition anthology and on The Poetry Society website.

Pascale Petit on Dom Bury's 'The Opened Field'
'The Opened Field' is a neutron star of a poem compressed inside the restraining machinery of a sestina. It's a dark allegory of six boys in a field, but I did not realise it was a sestina until a second reading, when I started to work out what the boys were up to, and what part the far from passive field was playing in these coming-of-age rituals with their compelling rhythm and mantra-like repetitions. The form is a perfect container for the interlinked themes: an interrogation of unchecked masculinity and our destructive relationship with each other and with the natural world. The barbaric impulses enacted are interwoven to offer us a sombre and precisely wrought fable for our times. That farm animals are involved is significant and points to a visionary eco-poetics. I marvelled at the way I found yet another layer each time I returned to this poem and still thought I had not quite got to the bottom of it. As the weeks passed it would haunt me like a recurring dream. Reading it aloud at our judging meeting, I felt the hairs on the back of my neck rise. The poem's mnemonic force and seriousness drew it to the top of the pile, to become our winner.

Andrew McMillan on Mary Jean Chan's 'The Window'
Looking back over the notes I'd made on this poem on my first reading, I see I've put a huge tick next to it, and then written "I love this" at the side. This is a quite remarkable poem, heartbreaking and affirming in equal measure: it has the quality of a perfectly composed symphony – its balance between high language ("the slightest touch of grace") and plain insight which cuts through everything ("tell the one who / detests the queerness

in you"). As we were making our final decisions, someone read this poem aloud, and I wept. It is such a tender, beautiful poem, full of an aching, a yearning and yet a stillness too; as though standing at a high window, and looking outwards.

Hannah Lowe on Momtaza Mehri's 'Oiled Legs Have Their Own Subtext'
This incredibly rich and textured poem demanded reading again and again. It is accumulative in effect, skilfully selecting details and juxtaposing these to give a picture of a life or lives affected by war, violence and displacement. The burden of the past "to those born carrying history as an extra limb" spills into specific acts of violence – women setting themselves alight, detainees stitching their mouths shut. The form of the poem – a long prose poem of broken sections – suits this content perfectly. The poem's handling and descriptions of time are also skilful and poignant, suggesting the interminable nature of war and its effects – "the war that broke you / breaks ten years ahead / and you are the one drowning / you are forgotten / in this life". The poem is held together by its address to a specific yet amorphous "you", making the reader wonder who is being addressed here – a forebear, a friend, the speaker themselves?

. . .

National Poetry Competition 2017 Winners

First Prize: Dom Bury, 'The Opened Field'
Second Prize: Mary Jean Chan, 'The Window'
Third Prize: Momtaza Mehri, 'Oiled Legs Have Their Own Subtext'
Commended: Peter Kahn, 'Till It's Gone'
Commended: Joseph Butler, 'AngelBat'
Commended: Paul Talbot, 'Danube 1994'
Commended: David Grubb, 'Inventions at the Asylum'
Commended: Yvonne Reddick, 'Muirburn'
Commended: Robert Powell, 'The Telling'
Commended: Jane Slavin, 'Perishable Goods'

DOM BURY

The Opened Field

Six boys, a calf's tongue each, one task –
to gulp each slick muscle down in turn,
to swallow each vein whole and not give
back a word, a sign, our mothers' names.
The scab stripped off, the ritual learned –
five boys step out across an empty field.

Five boys step out across an empty field
to find a fire already made, the task
to dock then brand a single lamb. We learnt
fast how to hold, then cut, then turn
each tail away, to print in them our names –
our ownership. We dock, we brand, give

iron to the skin until at last their legs give.
Four boys step out across an empty field,
each small child waiting for a name,
our own name to be called, the next task
ours to own, ours to slice into, to turn
each blade, to shear off skin until we learnt

the weight of it. One by one we learnt
the force our bodies hold, the subtle give
our own hands have, how not to turn
our gaze. Three boys stand in a frozen field –
each child stripped and hosed, the next task
not to read the wind but learn the names

we have for snow, each name
we have given to the world. To then unlearn
ourselves, the self, this is – the hardest task.
To have nothing left. No thing but heat to give.
Two boys step out across an empty field.
Still waiting for the call, waiting for our turn,

waiting to become, to dig, to turn
at last our hands into the soil then name
the weakest as an offering – the field
opened to a grave, my last chore not to learn
the ground but taste it closed. I don't give
back a word, surprise I am the task

that what the land gives it must then learn
to turn back into soil. One child, a name its task
to steal. Five boys turn from an empty field.

MARY JEAN CHAN

The Window
after Marie Howe

Once in a lifetime, you will gesture
at an open window, tell the one who
detests the queerness in you that *dead
daughters do not disappoint*, free your
sore knees from inching towards a kind
of reprieve, declare yourself genderless
as hawk or sparrow: an encumbered body
let loose from its cage. You will refuse your
mother's rage, her spit, her tongue heavy
like the heaviest of stones. Your mother's
anger is like the sun, which is like love,
which is the easiest thing – even on the
hardest of days. You will linger, knowing
that this standing before an open window
is what the living do, that they sometimes
reconsider at the slightest touch of grace.

MOMTAZA MEHRI

Oiled Legs Have Their Own Subtext

doctor says there is something wrong with your thyroid / you are known
to leak everywhere / to take the shape of whatever / wherever you are
poured into / you do not contest his claim / or any other man with his
hands around your throat / before the appointment / you slice a heart /
swallow breath mints to disguise / the miasma of desperation / slide a
ring onto each finger / bejewel a somatic distraction / let the Gulf of Aden
run ragged / from the twinned lakes / of shoulder blades / an inherited
wetness behind the ears / you kiss / the mirror's cold navel / with the kind
of pride that comes naturally / to those born carrying history as an extra
limb / to the sticky yolk of grief / you do not think you are a Good Person™
/ not with the way you cough up contradiction / phlegm thick as Aramco
/ poverty's slick jaw / or how you gloss your mouth with a humanitarian
shade of pink / dress each lie in crushed pearls / but because you
remember the names of your brothers / never your sisters / your sister's
sisters / your sisters who are an occurrence / never an event / never a
shudder when they stop occurring / there is nothing to mark their arrival
/ or leaving / Hodan aged 21 / and six months / who doused herself in
liquid surrender / set herself alight / her second attempt at peace / in the
bulletin thumbnail she wears royal blue / looks like a woman you would
powder / your nose next to / at a wedding / wrist against cheek / soft wick
of her rimmed eyes / banjee queen / doe-eyed diva / dhow-hearted / what
did they do to you / onto you / at Nauru Regional Processing Centre / what
did this processing look like / OPC1 / where detainees sew their lips
together / silence themselves before they are silenced / where women
hoard cloths to plug their bleeding / hide from both inmates and guards
/ carry the children of men who did not ask / infants who did not ask / an
island of orphans / of what could have been you / but is not you / will
never be you / from across the ambit / oh for fate's insurgencies / its sweet
edge / the topologies of our lives / their sharpened sighs / soft implosions
of flip-flops / on airport floors / you dream in eastern time / wait for the
hijaz to collect / the bags under your eyes / for her to warm your pulse /
with her hands / her cratered lap / friends described her as a "gentle soul"

who had been "destroyed" / by her time in detention / you note the
alliterative phrasing / a velvet undoing / there are as many ways to be
destroyed / as there are droplets on the tongue / to describe it / Hodan
rolls in your mouth / draws salt from saliva / you think of the white of
nerve endings / the melting of dermis / grass hissing underfoot / all that
separates her / from / you / me / is a slip of a generation / a fistful of
decades / in another life / the war that broke you / breaks ten years ahead
/ and you are the one drowning / you are forgotten / in this life / you rest
on the pillow of abstraction / on your passport / the freedom papers of
this age / your proximity to the bodies that terrorise hers / the rolled dice
of your life / it is what it is / every poem that falls / chandeliered / is about
this distance / its heavy head on your lap / its hot laugh on your neck / its
doll-like teeth marks / you have never known a violence
/ worse / than / coincidence /

CONTRIBUTORS

Anthony Anaxagorou is a British-born Cypriot award-winning poet, fiction writer, essayist, publisher and poetry educator. He has published nine volumes of poetry • **Mona Arshi**'s *Small Hands* (Liverpool University Press, 2015) won the Forward Prize for Best First Collection • **Fiona Benson**'s second collection, *Vertigo & Ghost*, will be published by Cape in 2019 • **Alison Brackenbury**'s latest collection, with a selection of her grandmother's superb recipes, is *Aunt Margaret's Pudding*, due from HappenStance • **Paul Celan** (1920–1970) was a German-language poet and translator, born in Romania • **Don Mee Choi**'s most recent book is *Hardly War* (Wave, 2016). She has translated a number of Kim Hyesoon's books • **Wendy Cope**'s fifth collection is *Anecdotal Evidence* (Faber, 2018) • **Rebecca Goss**'s most recent collection is *Her Birth* (Carcanet, 2013), which was shortlisted for the Forward Prize • **W.S. Graham** (1918–1986) was born in Greenock, Scotland. His primary publisher is Faber & Faber • **Philip Gross**'s *A Bright Acoustic* was published by Bloodaxe in 2017 • **Choman Hardi** was born in Kurdistan-Iraq and sought asylum in the UK in 1993. She has published two collections of poetry with Bloodaxe and a book of translation with Arc • **Harmony Holiday**'s latest book is *Hollywood Forever* (Fence, 2017). She lives in Los Angeles • **Kim Hyesoon** is an award-winning South Korean poet. The most recent English translation of her work (by Don Mee Choi) is *I'm OK, I'm Pig!* (Bloodaxe, 2014) • **Carolyn Jess-Cooke**'s most recent works include *Writing Motherhood: A Creative Anthology* (Seren, 2017) and *I Know My Name* (HarperCollins, 2017) • **Pierre Joris** is a Luxembourg-American poet, translator and essayist. He has translated much of Celan's work • **Igor Klikovac** is a Bosnian poet who has lived in London since 1993. A selection from his third book, *Stockholm Syndrome*, translated with John McAuliffe, will be published later this year with Smith|Doorstop • **Fran Lock** is the author of four books. Her most recent is *Muses & Bruises* (Manifesto Press, 2017) • **Hannah Lowe**'s latest collection is *Chan* (Bloodaxe, 2016). She is the current poet-in-residence at Keats House and teaches Creative Writing at Brunel University • **John McAuliffe**'s fourth book *The Way In* (Gallery) was joint winner of the 2016 Michael Hartnett Award for Best Collection • **Ruth McIlroy** was a winner of The Poetry Business International Book and Pamphlet Competition 2016/17 • **Andrew McMillan**'s second collection, *playtime* (Cape, 2018), appears in August • **Kathryn Maris**'s third collection, *The House with Only an Attic and a Basement* (Penguin, 2018), is forthcoming • **Ange Mlinko**'s fifth collection of poetry, *Distant Mandate*, was published this year by Farrar, Straus and Giroux • **Doireann Ní Ghríofa** is a bilingual Irish poet whose awards include the Rooney Prize for Irish Literature, and a Seamus Heaney Fellowship • **Jack Nicholls** is from Cornwall. He is the author of the pamphlet *Meat Songs* (The Emma Press, 2017) • **Ruth Padel**'s eleventh collection, *Emerald*, will be out in July. She is Professor of Poetry at King's College London • **Lawrence Sail**'s most recent collection is *The Quick* (Bloodaxe, 2015). *Guises*, a new collection, is due next year • **Jack Underwood**'s debut collection *Happiness* (Faber, 2015) won the Somerset Maugham Award.

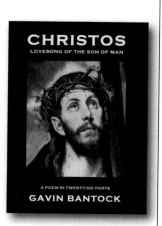